SERIOUSLY SIMPLE HOLIDAYS

SERIOUSLY SIMPLE HOLIDAYS

RECIPES AND IDEAS
TO CELEBRATE THE SEASON

by Diane Rossen Worthington
author of *Seriously Simple*

Wine Recommendations by Peter Marks

Photographs by Noel Barnhurst

CHRONICLE BOOKS
SAN FRANCISCO

Library of Congress Cataloging-in-Publication Data available.

ISBN-10: 0-8118-5480-9
ISBN-13: 978-0-8118-5480-1

Manufactured in China

Design and typesetting by Katie Heit
Food and Prop Stylist: George Dolese
Photographer's Assistants: Sara Johnson Loehmann and Samantha Rhea Lawson
Associate Food Stylist: Elisabet der Nederlanden

PHOTOGRAPHER'S ACKNOWLEDGMENTS:
Noel Barnhurst would like to thank his studio staff for their
continued hard work and good humor.

Distributed in Canada by Raincoast Books
9050 Shaughnessy Street
Vancouver, British Columbia V6P 6E5

10 9 8 7 6 5 4 3 2 1

Chronicle Books LLC
680 Second Street
San Francisco, California 94107
www.chroniclebooks.com

For my Mom, Ruth Rossen, who always made holidays special

———

ACKNOWLEDGMENTS

Ethan Ellenberg, my agent, who is always there with a creative thought

Bill LeBlond, my incredibly supportive editor, who is always available
to listen to my ideas

Amy Treadwell, for her helpful editorial input and her patience in answering my
questions and helping me solve organizational challenges

Juli Tantum, who had a big hand in this book, for her accomplished culinary
expertise, research, and writing and editing skills

Peter Marks, MW, director of wine at Copia, who brought his expert knowledge
to the wine-pairing advice

Fran McCullough, my friend and editor, who helped me create
the term "Seriously Simple"

Laurie Burrows Grad, Andy and Kathy Blue, Janice Wald Henderson, Jan Weimer,
and Ciji Ware, my cooking colleagues and dear friends, for all of their input

My brothers Richard and Bob Rossen for their sense of humor and support

Denny Luria; Mary Beth Rose; Connie Bryson; Judy Miller; Midori Firestone;
Virginia Paca; Lisa and Steve Hillman; Cathi, George, Lucy, and Harry
Rimalower; and Michael Schneider for being great tasters and critics

And last but not least, my husband Michael and my daughter Laura,
my biggest critics and my biggest fans

TABLE OF CONTENTS

INTRODUCTION

Autumn is an exciting time of year, as we transition from lazy summer days to the hustle and bustle of the holidays to come. There is a nip in the air, trees are aglow with colorful leaves, and school is swinging back into gear. Inside, the routines of fall and comforting foods of the season welcome cooks back into the kitchen.

I relish this flurry of activity after summer vacation. Autumn and winter are exhilarating, and I look forward to preparations for all the holidays that occur from September through January. So I take stock of my pantry and make room for the ingredients I like to have on hand in the cooler months. Markets begin to burst with fall's harvest—golden pears, crisp apples, dark maple syrup, bags of fresh cranberries, colorful squashes—and as I walk through the aisles, I feel inspired by the season's bounty.

But as I dream about heartier entrées and holiday gatherings, I give myself a dose of reality. I look at these meals from a different perspective—that of someone who has limited time, yet a great desire to entertain.

What we need are new strategies for entertaining that fit our busy lifestyles.

Recognizing this, I have stuck to my underlying philosophy of sophisticated simplicity. In my previous book, *Seriously Simple*, my focus was on flavor, quality ingredients, and presentation, with an emphasis on simplicity. My mission is the same in this book. The recipes are designed to reduce prep time and streamline cooking techniques while ensuring the high quality of the finished dish. Most holiday foods need a few more ingredients than summery grill foods to achieve depth of flavor. This doesn't mean you'll spend many hours in the kitchen. Turkey and Pinto Bean Chili (page 124); Mediterranean-Style Chicken with Capers, Plums, and

Olives (page 107); and Cornbread, Oyster, and Red Pepper Stuffing (page 186) may look like long recipes, but putting the dishes together couldn't be easier. You'll also find cooking tricks to shave off minutes without compromising flavor.

A notable change has occurred in the four years since I wrote *Seriously Simple*. The food industry has responded to the home cook's desire for simplicity by creating an array of quality prepared foods. Serious cooks are relying on these convenience ingredients to save time in the kitchen. Store shelves are now filled with beautiful jams and compotes, artisan cheeses, bags of precut vegetables, flavorful salsas, and bottles of pomegranate juice. A savvy cook can turn out an impressively rich Butternut Squash Lasagna (page 172) in record time by purchasing bags of already cubed squash and packages of precooked lasagna noodles.

I have taken advantage of quality prepared foods in many of my recipes by combining them with seasonal produce. Using a variety of the freshest ingredients with pantry-ready flavor enhancers, along with time-saving cooking techniques, makes for sophisticated simplicity during the holidays. "Appetizers from the Market to the Table" (page 62) captures the idea of convenience foods used with fresh foods in imaginative ways.

Whether it's a Thanksgiving feast, a last-minute casual get-together, or an elegant Christmas Eve dinner, I take pleasure in the planning, shopping, and food preparation. For me, Seriously Simple Holidays mean beautifully presented food that speaks for itself. There is no need to set elaborate tables. Think of the food as your centerpiece. Just remember that less is more when it comes to setting your table. Here are some of my guidelines for making it all possible.

THE HOLIDAY PANTRY IS ESSENTIAL.

The book opens with a peek into my "seasonal cupboard" of ingredients that I like to stock. If I have candied nuts, fresh goat cheese, apples, and lettuce, tossing together a Winter Chopped Salad (page 80) is a breeze. Guests won't notice that the deceptively easy Citrus-Glazed Chicken with Artichoke Hearts and Thyme (page 109) is made with frozen artichoke hearts. Roast Loin of Pork with Mustard Crust (page 145) is rubbed with mustard that I have on hand. My Seriously Simple condiments— Seriously Simple Seasoning Salt (page 208) and Balsamic Glaze (page 209)—are always within reach, especially for dishes that use just a few ingredients. These highly concentrated flavor boosters quickly add depth to a dish and take it from ordinary to memorable.

ADVANCE PLANNING AND ORGANIZATION ARE ESSENTIAL.

When time is of the essence, planning and cooking ahead are the secrets to pulling off great meals. You don't have to be a gourmet cook to host a great celebration, but you do need to be organized. In the following pages I give you tips on how to plan, make lists, shop ahead, and cook in advance so holiday gatherings happen with ease. Having a clear game plan is essential for creating clever, flavorful meals. Many of the dishes in this book can be prepared ahead and frozen or refrigerated until ready to serve. Most of the soups and baked pastas are ideal for freezing, as are such dishes as Spicy Sausage and Chicken Liver Pâté (page 52) and Pumpkin-Caramel Ice Cream Pie (page 195). Some components of recipes can be made a few days ahead and refrigerated, like salad dressings, marinades, or the bases for Cioppino (page 160) and Holiday Seafood Gumbo (page 157). Even Savory Bread Pudding with Bacon, Peppers, and Spinach (page 90) and Chocolate-Chip Pecan Crumb Coffee Cake (page 94) can be baked several hours ahead and reheated.

QUICK RECIPES ARE NECESSARY FOR LAST-MINUTE MEALS.

Since the holidays are often about dropping in on friends and family, I include several recipes that can be assembled on short notice. These exceedingly easy recipes have clear instructions to guide even the most basic cook. If friends drop by for breakfast, Breakfast Crostini (page 96) is just the thing. Chicken Paillards with Cranberry-Port Sauce (page 106) is the essence of holiday flavors, yet can be tossed together in minutes. If you have time to stop at the market to purchase a piece of fresh wild salmon, Slow-Roasted Salmon with Miso Vinaigrette (page 151) requires just a few steps once you arrive home. Other especially easy seafood recipes are Roasted Halibut with Pistachio-Parmesan Crust (page 152) and Glazed Whitefish with Red Pepper Aioli (page 153).

TAKE ADVANTAGE OF SHORTCUTS WHEREVER POSSIBLE.

Being aware of simplified techniques can streamline cooking holiday meals. For Holiday Seafood Gumbo (page 157), I make a dark roux in the microwave instead of stirring it over the stove for the usual forty-five minutes. Store-bought trail mix shows up as a convenient surprise ingredient in the Sausage, Dried Fruit, and Nut Stuffing (page 187).

REINVENT CLASSIC DISHES TO KEEP THEM SIMPLE BUT STILL DELICIOUS.

Updating traditional recipes is another big component of Seriously Simple entertaining during the holidays. Brisket with Figs and Butternut Squash (page 130) uses figs and squash instead of traditional red wine sauce. I created the "Pasta, Vegetables, and Side Dishes" section specifically with casual, family-style entertaining in mind. These recipes are variations of family favorites, such as Perfect Mashed Potatoes (page 185), and Polenta with Butternut Squash and Chestnuts (page 182).

I loved doing the dessert chapter since most of the recipes are rustic renditions of classic dishes, and I was able to highlight the season through ingredients like dried fruits, pumpkin, and persimmons. Dried Fruit and Chocolate Bar Cookies (page 197) are my version of a fruitcake reincarnated as something you would actually enjoy eating. Sour Cream–Vanilla Cupcakes (page 198) can be served plain or decorated with holiday flair for family gatherings with children.

With these guiding principles in mind, I've created new recipes suited to the fall and winter holidays. Since I am always looking for fresh ways to cook a dish, I've once again included "The Clever Cook Could" features throughout the book to encourage you to change a recipe on your own. These suggestions will give you the freedom and confidence to adapt a dish to suit your taste or the occasion.

With the festivities of fall and winter holidays come ample opportunities for gift giving. I've developed a section called "Gifts from the Kitchen," full of easy, clever recipes to cook ahead and wrap as gifts.

Many holiday occasions—celebratory family feasts, lavish cocktail parties, fireside picnics—call for serving drinks. The book has a section of holiday drink recipes. In addition, wine expert Peter Marks gives thoughtful wine recommendations for all of the entrées. Peter, who has qualified as a Master of Wine, has an extensive food background. Guided by Peter's expertise, cooks will be able to choose appropriate drinks and not be overwhelmed while planning menus.

At this time of the year when meals are special, cooks have grand visions and a great desire to entertain. The hard part is being realistic about what they can accomplish. It is my hope that the following recipes leave you plenty of time to enjoy yourself as well as please your guests. Always remember that a good holiday party requires two main ingredients—good friends and good food.

—*Diane Rossen Worthington*

The Holiday Pantry

The contents of my holiday pantry look very similar to the items in my year-round pantry with an array of notable additions. These are among the ingredients I make sure I have on hand for cooking my recipes.

———

APPLE BRANDY
Use a domestic variety for cooking.

APPLES
An important component of cold-weather cooking.
- FUJI: Firm and sweet, ideal for salads and applesauce and for baking.
- GALA: Vibrant red and yellow, excellent for general cooking and baking.
- GOLDEN DELICIOUS: Firm flesh with rich, mellow flavor. I like to use this variety in pies, relishes, and sauces.
- PINK LADY: Crisp and dense, wonderful for eating fresh and for baking.
- PIPPIN AND GRANNY SMITH: Tart and firm. Hold up well when baked, notably in pies.

ARTICHOKE HEARTS
Choose good-quality frozen hearts and defrost for use in salads and chicken dishes or as an appetizer.

BACON
Look for applewood-smoked bacon for its delicious flavor. You can substitute uncured bacon.

BEANS
Rinse all canned beans and drain before using.
- CANNED GARBANZO BEANS: Also called chickpeas. Excellent in salads and soups.
- CANNED PINTO BEANS: For making chili and other soups and stews.

BELGIAN ENDIVE
Belonging to the chicory family, this tight, cream-and-red head has a slightly bitter flavor. Endives are excellent in salads or cooked as a vegetable. Store in the refrigerator.

BROTHS AND STOCKS
Chicken, beef, fish, and vegetable broths are available in cartons, which I prefer over the cans so that

leftovers can be refrigerated in the container. Look for low-salt and fat-free varieties. I keep frozen containers of both fish and veal stock for last-minute cooking.

BUTTER
I use unsalted butter because it has no preservatives and has an excellent flavor. I keep a pound or two in my freezer at all times.

CABBAGE
Use green cabbage. Select heavy heads that have shiny leaves, and store in the refrigerator.

CANDY CANES
Use small peppermint-flavored candy canes for garnishing holiday desserts and for decorations.

CAPERS
Whether you choose the small French nonpareil variety packed in brine or the larger Italian capers, rinse them well to remove excess brine or salt. They add a piquant flavor to salads, dressings, and sauces, and make a simple garnish.

CHAMPAGNE
True Champagne comes only from the Champagne region of France. Sparkling wines, as many other varieties are called, vary in color from pale gold to apricot, and range in flavor from dry (no sugar) to sweet (dessert wines). Brut or extra-dry levels of sweetness are best for cocktail sipping.

CHEESE
- BLUE: Several varieties are good choices, such as American Maytag blue and Point Reyes blue and imported Gorgonzola, Stilton, and Roquefort.
- GOAT: Once available only from France, fresh goat cheese, or chèvre, is now produced by small cottage industries across the United States. The American version is slightly milder than European goat cheese. Fresh goat cheese has a soft texture similar to that of cream cheese. It is good served warm over salad or as an ingredient in cold salads and pasta sauces. As goat cheese ages, it becomes stronger and its character more pronounced.
- MASCARPONE: Cow's milk cheese that must be eaten very fresh. This delicious creamy dessert cheese is a bit like whipped butter or stiffly whipped cream. It is often sweetened slightly and served with fresh fruit and added to dishes as a flavor enhancer. Look for the Italian or domestic variety sold in small tubs.
- MOZZARELLA: Most regular mozzarella in supermarkets is low-fat or nonfat. It has a semisoft, elastic texture and is drier and not as delicately flavored as its fresh counterpart. This style of mozzarella is best used for cooking and is popular for pizza or pasta dishes because of its excellent melting qualities.
- PARMESAN: Authentic Italian Parmigiano-Reggiano comes from the region of Emilia-Romagna, where it is strictly licensed and has been produced in much the same way for almost 700 years. The cheese should be straw yellow in color with a crumbly, moist texture. Look for the words *Parmigiano-Reggiano*

stamped on the rind. Store wrapped in plastic in the refrigerator for up to 3 weeks. It's best to grate Parmesan as needed for the best flavor.

* RICOTTA: Smooth and milky tasting, this Italian fresh, unripened cheese is made from the whey of cow's milk or sheep's milk, depending on the regional version. A low-fat variety is often available.

CHESTNUTS
A delicious addition to stuffings, soups and stews, or sauces. Look for cooked and peeled chestnuts in jars.

CHIPOTLE CHILES
Smoked, dried jalapeños, chipotles are available canned in a sauce of garlic, tomatoes, and vinegar, labeled "chipotles en adobo." Moderately hot, they have a distinctive smoky flavor.

CHOCOLATE
Store all solid chocolate in a cool, dark place.

* BITTERSWEET AND SEMISWEET: Bittersweet chocolate usually has 70 to 75 percent cacao. Semi-sweet chocolate usually has 60 percent cacao. For bittersweet or semisweet chocolate I use imported Valrhona or Callebaut or domestic Scharffen Berger or Ghirardelli.
* COCOA POWDER: Select the sweetened variety. Ghirardelli and Scharffen Berger make cocoa powder sweetened with sugar, which eliminates one step in making hot chocolate. Do not confuse this product

with instant cocoa mix, a combination of cocoa powder, milk powder, and sugar.

* UNSWEETENED: Chocolate liquor with no added sugar, used in baking to flavor items that have other sources of sweetness. I like Scharffen Berger, Baker's, and Hershey's.
* WHITE: Contains cocoa butter but no chocolate liquor, which is what gives chocolate its bitter, intense chocolate flavor and color. I like Ghirardelli and Lindt. Use for baking cakes, cookies, and muffins.

COGNAC
Considered the finest of all brandies. I use a VSOP for cooking.

COINTREAU
Light, not too sweet orange-flavored liqueur for cooking and drinking.

COOKING OIL SPRAY

Both olive oil and vegetable oil sprays save calories, time, and cleanup. You can also buy a baking spray that combines oil and flour.

CORN

Select sweet corn kernels that have been picked and frozen at their peak of freshness. Good to have on hand to add to polenta or cornbread.

CORNMEAL

A medium to coarsely ground variety is recommended.

CRANBERRIES

Bright red and very tart, cranberries are a favorite complement to heavy meats and poultry because the berry's acidity works well against the fattiness. Choose firm, plump fresh cranberries with a glossy luster. Discard those that are blemished or discolored. Since cranberries are in season for only a few months, buy a few extra bags to freeze for up to a year. But don't defrost the berries before you cook them. They will better retain their firmness if cooked frozen.

CREMINI MUSHROOM

Type of button mushroom that is brown and has a richer flavor than the white button mushroom. When grown to its full size, it becomes a portobello mushroom. Store in a paper bag in the refrigerator.

CURLY ENDIVE

A compact lettuce with slightly bitter leaves ideal for salads. Store this member of the chicory family in the refrigerator.

DATES

Most varieties are available year-round, with supplies peaking October to December. I like Medjool dates for use as an appetizer, in salads, and in bread puddings and other desserts. Store dates in a tightly closed container in the refrigerator.

DRIED FRUITS

Dried cranberries, cherries, apricots, figs, currants, and plums are good pantry items in the winter months when fresh fruit is not abundant. Add them to rice pudding, savory sauces, rice, and stuffings. Dried cranberries can be used like raisins in baking and cooking. I like to plump them in boiling water or wine to bring out their full flavor.

DRIED HERBS

Have on hand basil, thyme, rosemary, and oregano; look for the whole-leaf variety.

DRIED MUSHROOMS

I like to use shiitake, porcini, or morel. They need to be rehydrated before using. Make sure the mushrooms are tightly packaged, protected from moisture, before purchasing.

FIGS

Fresh figs are available in the fall months. Look for Mission, with a deep purple-black skin; Kadota, with yellow-green skin; Brown Turkey, with a brownish purple skin; or Calimyrna, a pale yellow color. Any of these varieties is excellent for cooking or eating raw. Refrigerate until using.

FLOUR

I prefer unbleached all-purpose flour for general baking and other uses.

FRUIT NECTARS

I like to use guava, apricot, and peach nectars for drinks. Their concentrated flavor is also excellent for marinades.

GARLIC CLOVES, PEELED

You can find this product in the refrigerated produce section. Using already peeled cloves will save you time, especially when you need large quantities. Make sure to cut off the root ends to avoid bitterness.

GINGER

Fresh ginger, also called gingerroot, is a knobby-looking tuber with smooth, golden skin. Used extensively in Chinese and Japanese cooking, ginger has become a common ingredient in American cooking. It should be peeled, then may be shredded, grated, or cut into julienne strips. Do not substitute dried ginger.

HONEY

The many types of honey vary in flavor and appearance, ranging from thin to almost hard, and white to golden and amber to varnish brown or even black. The most popular types are clover honey and orange honey, both of which are suitable for cooking and baking. Look for lavender, sage, white truffle, or wildflower honey at specialty-food stores and farmers' markets. All honeys should be stored in tightly sealed containers, although eventually they will crystallize and harden. To soften the honey, place the jar in a bowl of hot water.

HORSERADISH

I like cream-style horseradish. Use it to flavor sauces.

JALAPEÑO CHILE

This bright green, 1½-inch-long chile ranges from hot to very hot and is one of the most widely used in the United States. It is available canned or fresh and is sometimes seen fresh in its bright red ripe state. When you're working with chiles, always wear rubber gloves. Wash the cutting surface and knife immediately.

LEMON

One of the most versatile citrus fruits, lemons have many culinary uses, so it's good to keep lots on hand. If you can find Meyer lemons, they add a wonderful sweet accent to dishes. A few drops of fresh lemon juice can enhance poultry, fish, vegetables, and baked foods, and the acid can prevent fruits from turning brown when exposed to air. The outer layer of the peel is often grated and used for flavoring. Fresh lemon juice is preferred over bottled.

LIME
Slightly sweeter than lemons, limes are good to have in stock for juices, cocktails, preserves, salsas, and salads.

MAPLE SYRUP
Pure maple syrup gives a deep, complex sweetness to a variety of dishes, both savory and sweet. I like good-quality, dark amber Grade B syrup for cooking as the flavor is more intense than the light Grade A, which is best for pouring over pancakes. Look for pure maple syrup from producers in Canada, Vermont, or New Hampshire. I use maple syrup in salad dressing, baked beans, nut tarts, plain yogurt, or warm cereal as well as to garnish pancakes and waffles and to sweeten muffins or coffee cake.

MATZO MEAL
Unleavened bread called matzo is ground to make matzo meal. It is great for stuffing and as a substitute for bread crumbs, and is essential for preparing matzo balls.

MISO
Soybean paste that comes in several varieties. I use white miso (actually a pale yellow), also called *shiro miso*, for its slightly sweet flavor. Look for miso in the refrigerated section of supermarkets or in Asian markets. Miso is good in sauces, dressings, and marinades.

MUSTARDS
I like to keep three different mustards on hand.
* DIJON: Smooth, silky textured, and slightly tangy. Grey Poupon is a good brand.
* HONEY: Make sure this version has a base of Dijon mustard and is not the ballpark variety.
* WHOLE GRAIN: Includes mustard seeds that have not been ground.

NUTS
Purchase raw nuts in quantity and store in a lock-top plastic bag in the freezer.
* ALMONDS: Select blanched whole or slivered almonds.
* CANDIED PECANS OR WALNUTS: Great to have on hand for salads and appetizers.
* MARCONA ALMONDS: Delicious flavored Spanish almond that is a great companion to cocktails.
* PECANS: Select pecan halves.

- PISTACHIOS: Look for raw, shelled, unsalted green pistachios, available in most supermarkets.
- WALNUTS: Select walnut halves.

OATMEAL

Quick-cooking steel-cut Irish oatmeal, which has more texture than traditional oatmeal, is great for quick breakfasts.

OLIVE OIL

There are many types of olive oils, each possessing different characteristics based on the olive variety, growing conditions such as climate and soil, and the amount of processing involved.

- EXTRA-VIRGIN: This cold-pressed oil is rich and full flavored, usually fruity, green, and redolent of olives. It is wonderful when used unheated as a flavoring agent in salad dressings or drizzled over vegetables or bread. Many varieties are available so try a few until you find your favorite. Some are milder and can be used in cooking.
- PURE: Made from olives that have been heated and pressed to extract the last bit of oil. Pure oils are milder than extra-virgin. I use them for sautéing because their flavor won't overwhelm the dish.

OLIVES

- GREEN: Select mild, pitted French olives in jars for use in tapenade, salads, and chicken dishes and as an appetizer.
- KALAMATA: These almond-shaped Greek olives are rich, salty, and slightly fruity in flavor. They are soaked in a wine vinegar marinade and sold in jars either with the pits intact or pitted.

ONIONS AND OTHER AROMATICS

- CHIVE: Delicate, dark green herb in the onion family with a mild flavor. For maximum flavor, slice the leaves finely and sprinkle over potatoes, light pasta, and salads just before serving. Chives are an excellent garnish on any dish that contains onion.
- GARLIC: A seasoning enhancer whose intense flavor and fragrance mellow when cooked. A bulb is composed of at least 20 cloves.
- LEEK: My favorite member of the onion family for its natural sweetness and its ability to stand alone as an elegant side dish. Ideal in soups, stews, and sauces as well. To prepare, cut off the dark green top and score the leek lengthwise, stopping before the root end. Rinse under cold running water.
- RED: Colorful and, like scallions, best served uncooked. Delicious when marinated with wine vinegar and cucumbers.
- SCALLION: Immature onions that have not fully developed a bulb. Common in Asian dishes and salads and as a garnish for soups, scallions are best served raw or lightly stir-fried. For a quick garnish, try clipping the scallion with scissors. Also called green onion.
- SHALLOT: Small onion with a concentrated flavor. I like to use shallots in sauces and also glazed whole.

- YELLOW AND WHITE: Most common cooking onions, appreciated for their relatively mild flavor. Use to season stews and soups, sauces, and meats.

ORANGES

Choose Valencia for juicing and navel for peeling and eating. The zest adds an extra orange flavor to any dish that contains orange juice or flesh. Oranges are great for last-minute desserts, and the juice is excellent in dressings, sauces, and marinades.

PANCETTA

The same cut as bacon, but salted, lightly spiced, and then cured, rather than smoked. It can be ordered cubed or sliced either thick or thin. American bacon may be substituted if necessary.

PANKO

Japanese bread crumbs—actually dried, toasted flakes—which are larger and coarser than Western-style crumbs. Available in plastic bags or jars in supermarkets and Asian markets.

PASTA, DRIED

Have on hand penne, fusilli, spaghetti, tagliatelle, and linguine, preferably an imported durum-wheat pasta from Italy like De Cecco. No-boil lasagna noodles, which have been precooked, come dried or refrigerated.

PEARS

At their peak throughout the winter, pears ripen best off the tree, so they are picked when still hard. Once they ripen, refrigerate them.

- ANJOU: Hold up well when cooked or baked. Also good sliced for salads.
- ASIAN OR JAPANESE: Crisp and juicy, with a sweet floral fragrance. Excellent for eating fresh as well as for cheese plates and salads.
- BARTLETT: All-purpose pear, ideal for cooking and eating fresh.
- BOSC: Distinctive brown skin and sweet cream-colored flesh. Terrific for poaching, baking, and eating fresh.
- COMICE: Favorite pear for eating fresh.
- SECKEL: Small and ideal for preserves or as decoration in centerpieces and floral arrangements.

PEPPER

Always use freshly ground black pepper, whether a recipe calls for this ingredient coarsely cracked or finely ground. I use ground white pepper especially with light-colored sauces.

PEPPERMINT EXTRACT

Good for adding to hot chocolate and for flavoring chocolate desserts.

PERSIMMONS

Their pleasant taste has been likened to the flavor of a ripe apricot.

- FUYU: Resembles a squat apple. This variety can be eaten out of hand like a crisp-hard apple off the tree; there is no need to cook them. They are great in salads and as a fruit topping.
- HACHIYA: Elongated, with a pointed tip. Should not be eaten until very soft, since they sweeten

as they ripen. The pulp is excellent in puddings and bread.

PETITS POIS
Tiny peas frozen at their peak so they maintain their shape and flavor in cooking.

POLENTA
A type of meal ground from sweet corn or maize. Instant (precooked) polenta has a finer texture and takes just minutes to cook.

POMEGRANATE
Available in October and November, pomegranates have a tangy, sweet flavor. The ruby red seeds are great for salads, sauces, and drinks. To harvest the seeds, score the skin from top to bottom into four quarters. Be careful not to puncture the fruit in order to maintain the integrity of the seeds. Separate the quarters and remove the tiny red seeds. I like to hold each quarter over a bowl and tap a wooden spoon on the skin side to release the seeds. This method also keeps my hands clean. The seeds make a beautiful accent for everything from salads and game roasts to desserts. Whole pomegranates are attractive in centerpieces and wreaths, especially when they begin to dry.

POMEGRANATE JUICE
Use the refrigerated sweetened variety.

PORT
Use a tawny port for cooking.

POTATOES
The ultimate comfort food, potatoes come in different colors and textures.

- FINGERLING AND BABY DUTCH: Delicious brushed with a bit of olive oil and roasted at high heat until creamy on the inside and browned and crisp on the exterior.
- RED AND WHITE: Good for roasting and in stews because they keep their waxy texture. Also delicious in mashed potatoes, although not quite as creamy as Yukon Gold or Yellow Finn.
- RUSSET: Also called Idaho or baking potato. This variety, with its starchy texture, is good for baking and in gratins because it soaks up liquid and becomes creamy.
- YELLOW FINN AND YUKON GOLD: Their rich flavor and consistency are excellent in just about any potato preparation.

PROSCIUTTO

Salt-cured ham that is neither cooked nor smoked. Ask for imported Italian prosciutto. For cooking, have it sliced 1/16 to 1/8 inch thick; any thinner and it will fall apart. However, it should be sliced paper-thin for serving draped over fruit.

RICE

Long-grain white rice cooks into separate and fluffy grains and is perfect for rice pilaf.

ROASTED PEPPERS

Sweet roasted red or yellow bell peppers in a jar packed in water, chopped or whole. Rinse and drain well before using in appetizers, sauces, pastas, or eggs.

RUM

Choose light rum for holiday drinks.

SAKE

Wine made from rice and water, and good in marinades for its unusual flavor. Look for an inexpensive variety with an alcohol content between 10 and 20 percent.

SALT

I like fine-grained sea salt and kosher salt because their flavor is superior to that of regular iodized table salt.

SATSUMAS

Available November through January, these small, sweet oranges are usually seedless and have skin that slides right off the flesh. Ideal for salads and whenever mandarin oranges would be used. Satsumas are often sold with stems and leaves attached, so bowls of the fruits make quick, colorful centerpieces.

SERIOUSLY SIMPLE SEASONING SALT

Versatile seasoning for use in general cooking and also as a rub. See recipe on page 208.

SOUR CREAM OR CRÈME FRAÎCHE

I keep both in my refrigerator for use in sauces and as a garnish. Light sour cream may be substituted in many dishes.

SOY SAUCE

Salty, dark brown condiment useful in marinades and sauces and as a flavor enhancer. I like the reduced-sodium variety.

SPICES

Allspice, ginger, cinnamon (ground and sticks), mulling spices, whole nutmegs, pumpkin pie spice, cayenne pepper, coriander, ground cumin, and red pepper flakes are the key spices to have for the holidays.

SUGAR

Stock granulated sugar for baking. You also can keep on hand ultrafine baking sugar and substitute it for granulated sugar. Powdered sugar, also called confectioners' sugar, is used for decorating desserts.

TOFFEE BITS

These come in bags and are a wonderful topping for ice cream or a flavorful addition to baked goods like cookies and brownies.

TOMATOES

* CANNED DICED, WITH JUICE: I use a good Italian variety or Muir Glen. For extra flavor, select the fire-roasted tomatoes.
* SUN-DRIED: Drying tomatoes greatly intensifies their flavor and gives them a chewy texture. Sun-dried tomatoes are available dried or packed in oil, halved or chopped.
* TOMATO PASTE: Buy in the tube imported from Italy so you can store it in the refrigerator.

TRAIL MIX

Combination of nuts and dried fruit that makes a good addition to stuffing. Look for mixes that contain only nuts and dried fruit.

VANILLA EXTRACT

Buy only a bottle labeled "pure vanilla"; I like the bold-flavored Tahitian pure vanilla.

VEGETABLE OIL

I like to use canola for its ability to withstand high temperatures and for its clean flavor.

VINEGARS

* BALSAMIC: Imported from Italy, true balsamic vinegar has a dark brownish red color and is slightly thicker than the usual red vinegar. For cooking, a commercial vinegar (versus the expensive artisan-produced vinegars) from Modena or nearby Reggio is fine. Look on the label for either API MO

(referring to Modena) or API RE (referring to Reggio) to be sure you aren't buying an imitation from another area. The flavor should have a refined sweet-tart balance.

* BALSAMIC GLAZE: If you don't have time to prepare the glaze, use a good-quality balsamic vinegar. See recipe on page 209.
* RED WINE: An aged vinegar made with good-quality grapes that has a full-bodied flavor.
* RICE: Chinese and Japanese products are milder and sweeter than regular distilled vinegars. They range in color from clear or golden to amber brown, and are available seasoned or sweetened with sugar. Good in salads, dressings, and sauces.
* SHERRY: Possessing a distinctive sherry-sweet and slightly tart flavor. Use in dressings and sauces.
* WHITE BALSAMIC: Produced by adding cooked-down grape juice to ordinary white wine vinegar, which gives it an amber color and slightly sweet flavor. Good in dressings and sauces.

WINE

For both cooking and drinking, have on hand a good medium-priced dry white wine, like Sauvignon Blanc or Chardonnay, and a good medium-priced red, such as Merlot or Zinfandel.

WINTER SQUASHES

Varying in size, shape, and color, they all have in common golden, velvety flesh with a rich, buttery taste. Their thick skin makes them a challenge to cut. Use a sharp swivel peeler to remove the thick, hard skin. A sharp knife also works well. Use winter squash in soups, pie fillings, vegetable gratins, and pizza toppings or as a colorful side, whether braised, roasted, steamed, or even microwaved.

Check out the unusual shapes and colors as the season evolves and use them as centerpieces and table ornaments at Halloween or Thanksgiving. Put them on your holiday table with pretty fall leaves, votive candles, and pinecones.

* ACORN: Resembling a giant acorn. Choose the green-skinned variety for its sweet flavor and less stringy flesh.
* BUTTERNUT: Looks like an elongated bell and is now available year-round. Great in soups and vegetable gratins, and on its own, steamed or puréed.
* HUBBARD: Excellent for baking and steaming.
* KABOCHA: Japanese squash with the texture of velvet. It is often deep-fried for tempura. I like to use it in soups.
* PUMPKIN: Small pumpkins (not miniatures) can be used in fillings and soups. For decorations, choose large specimens or baby pumpkins. Orange and white varieties of the latter are available. You can scoop them out and put a votive candle in them.

SHORTCUT INGREDIENTS FOR CLEVER COOKS

Set aside room in your pantry for some high-quality prepared ingredients. These can be a godsend to Seriously Simple home cooks since the chopping, peeling, and puréeing have already been done. Look for the items at supermarkets and specialty-food stores, on the shelves and in the refrigerator and freezer sections.

CHUTNEY: Spicy-sweet condiment that contains fruit, vinegar, sugar, and spices. It can be chunky or smooth, mild or hot, and serves as a great accompaniment to main dishes, cheese platters, and appetizers.

FIG COMPOTE: Made with dried figs, other dried fruits, sugar, and wine, this compote, sold in jars, is delicious with Brie and prosciutto as a sandwich or appetizer. Look for dark fig compotes or preserves that are on the thick side, with a true fig flavor; some can be overly sweet or too sour.

TAPENADE: Olive spread that usually combines olives, capers, anchovies, garlic, and olive oil. There are green and black olive varieties.

PESTO SAUCE: Select a full-flavored basil, spinach, or cilantro pesto. Buy the bottled variety or a refrigerated one.

SUN-DRIED TOMATO PESTO: Buy the bottled variety or a refrigerated one.

MARINARA SAUCE: Find an excellent bottled variety that you like.

MARINADES: Bottled marinades ready-to-go for chicken, fish, or meat.

DEMI-GLACE: Intensely flavored, thick, syrupy liquid made from long-simmered veal bones, vegetables, and seasonings. Purchase ready-made demi-glace in small tubs in stores or by mail order (Demi-Glace Gold, 800-860-9392).

SALSAS: Chipotle, tomatillo, and roasted tomato are among the available varieties. Serve with tortilla chips for a quick appetizer, stir into soups, or add to salad dressings. Try adding olive oil, lime juice, and garlic to create a marinade for fish or chicken. Look for the refrigerated salsas since they taste freshest.

PEELED AND CUT VEGETABLES: Bags of peeled, seeded, and cut vegetables, such as butternut squash and carrots, eliminate some prep work, while still retaining flavor and nutrition.

COLESLAW MIX: Bags of shredded cabbages, usually both red and green, sometimes with carrots, ready to use for coleslaw or to be sautéed as a side dish.

HUMMUS: Spread made from puréed garbanzo beans, tahini, garlic, and lemon juice, and sometimes roasted red peppers. Serve with warm pita triangles or crisp vegetables for an appetizer or spread on a sandwich.

Essential Holiday Equipment

Various key pieces of equipment are necessary for preparing holiday meals, especially Thanksgiving dinner. Even if you store some items away the rest of the year (like a fat separator), you will be glad to have them at your side for special meals.

―――――――――

BAKING PAN
9-by-13-inch, for cakes and puddings.

BAKING SHEET OR JELLY-ROLL PAN
For baking cookies, roasting meats and vegetables, and toasting nuts.

BASTING BRUSH OR BULB BASTER
To baste the turkey during roasting. Look for silicone brushes for ease in cleaning.

CARVING BOARD
Large wooden board with a trough for catching the juices.

CARVING KNIFE AND FORK
For the big moment. A good-quality, sharp knife will make the job much easier.

DUTCH OVEN
6-quart, for braising and cooking vegetables.

ELECTRIC MIXER
For making batters and other dessert preparations.

FAT SEPARATOR
For making gravy. The angled spout allows you to pour off the bottom layer of meat juices, leaving the fat behind.

FINE-MESH STRAINER
For straining gravy.

GRAVY BOAT
For serving gravy or sauces.

HAND BLENDER
Sometimes called an immersion blender, this device saves immeasurable cleanup time since you can purée right in the pot where the food is cooking. Excellent for soups.

HAND GRATER
Makes grating cheese or zesting citrus incredibly easy and fast. Look for different sizes for zesting and grating.

HEAVY-DUTY ALUMINUM FOIL
To cover the turkey during roasting.

HEAVY-DUTY ROASTING PAN WITH RACK
Keeps turkey slightly elevated for even cooking. If you use a foil roasting pan, nest two pans for extra strength.

INSTANT-READ THERMOMETER
No more questions about doneness with this accurate tool. Test for accuracy by dipping the tip in boiling water; it should read 212°F.

LARGE GLASS CLAMP JARS
For storing sauces in the refrigerator.

LARGE LIQUID MEASURING CUP
At least a 4-cup, preferably an 8-cup Pyrex.

LOCK-TOP PLASTIC BAGS
Large and jumbo sizes. Useful for marinating.

MINI FOOD PROCESSOR
For chopping garlic, shallots, parsley, and ginger, and for making fresh bread crumbs.

POTATO RICER OR POTATO MASHER
For mashing potatoes.

SAUCEPANS
2-, 3-, and 5-quart, for boiling, reheating, steaming, and sauce making.

SKILLET
12-inch, for sautéing large quantities of vegetables.

TONGS
I use various sizes for turning foods in hot pans and for sautéing.

VEGETABLE PEELER
Use a swivel peeler for ease in peeling. Look for a model with a serrated blade.

WIRE WHISK
For ensuring smooth gravy and pumpkin pie filling, and for whipping cream.

WOODEN SKEWERS
For trussing the turkey.

Holiday Entertaining Styles

Holiday meals can vary from intimate dinners to festive cocktail parties, and giving thought ahead of time to the layout of the meal will help guarantee a successful outcome. There is no magic formula, but the meal will appear to flow effortlessly with some advance planning.

BUFFET

When you decide to invite people to your home during the holidays, the trick to serving a crowd is to set up a dazzling buffet. With a little strategizing, this can be a truly simple way to entertain, since you are freed from most kitchen duties once the buffet is arranged and the guests have arrived. The beauty of a buffet is that you can supplement the dishes you make with quality prepared foods to create an abundant table.

A day or two ahead, think about which platters and bowls you will use and how the food will be displayed. Talented caterers have all kinds of tricks up their sleeves, like turning crates or boxes upside down and draping them with fabric or cloth napkins to create perches of varying height for platters. Baskets can be filled with rolls or utensils. Cake stands are an elegant way to present many kinds of food. I like to have several different sizes to provide height and interest to the table.

SIT-DOWN

For a group of four to twelve guests, a sit-down dinner is an intimate way to spend an evening. Plating the food in the kitchen allows you to cook dishes that don't work well on buffets, and to control the portions and presentation. Plan the menu so you aren't constantly jumping up from the table and spending the whole evening in the kitchen. Consider cooking a main course such as Baked Pasta with Tomato, Red Pepper, and Sweet Italian Sausage Sauce (page 169) or Braised Short Ribs with Guava Barbecue Sauce (page 136), which can be kept warm in the oven while you and your guests are having a first course.

FAMILY-STYLE

For holiday dinners at home, passing dishes around the table and letting guests serve themselves is a casual, fun way to entertain. Think ahead about the serving dishes and utensils you'll need, such as a small pair of tongs for picking up pieces of meat and spoons for ladling sauces. If foods are heavy and awkward, divide them among smaller serving dishes to facilitate passing. I like to place pitchers of water and wine bottles on the table so guests can help themselves throughout the meal.

POTLUCK

This style of entertaining can be a relaxing, inclusive way to entertain while allowing the host to focus on preparing a fabulous main dish, selecting interesting drinks, and decorating the table and house. Potlucks lend themselves well to spontaneous, communal gatherings and also to planned holidays such as Thanksgiving where guests often have a favorite family dish they like to share. But potlucks don't happen without a bit of strategy on the part of the host to ensure that the meal comes together in a balanced way.

For a potluck to be successful, the host needs to provide a certain amount of structure so guests don't arrive with three appetizers, several desserts, and no salads or vegetables. I like to offer choices (appetizer, salad, main dish, vegetable, dessert), and let guests tell me ahead of time what they would like to cook. If a guest is anxious about cooking, recommend an easy recipe or suggest bringing drinks. You can also build a potluck around a theme, such as an Italian dinner for Christmas Eve or a Mexican meal for football viewing.

Setting Up the Bar

The type of party you are giving will determine what you serve to drink and how much to buy. Whether the event is large or small, you need to plan ahead. In general I like to set up in advance and have it be as self-service as possible, so you don't have to spend all your time tending bar.

―――

I place pitchers of already mixed drinks alongside the glasses and ice, and set out opened wine bottles. For a large party, consider placing the bar in an area where you'd like guests to congregate (not necessarily in the kitchen), or creating two bars in separate areas to spread the party out.

Ice is inexpensive and easy to pick up beforehand, so be sure to purchase enough for chilling drinks. For a large cocktail party, fill a big metal or plastic tub with ice to chill white wine and sodas. This will free up your refrigerator for the food. If you're short on space and you have a big double sink, fill one side with ice for chilling drinks.

Having the right glasses is important, but they don't need to be the finest crystal. For a large party, you can often spend less to purchase inexpensive glasses from an outlet store or large home store than to rent them. I

like to use multipurpose wineglasses. You can keep the glasses stored away for the few times a year you need them, knowing that if one breaks it won't cost a fortune to replace.

ESSENTIAL BAR ITEMS

Remember to keep some items stocked at the bar so guests don't need to hunt through your drawers or cabinets to find them.

- Bottle openers for beer and wine
- Cocktail napkins
- Ice tongs and ice bucket
- Lemon and lime wedges
- Several clean towels for mopping up spills

I also like to place bowls of nuts and olives or a small tray of appetizers near the bar.

Gifts from the Kitchen

In the age of gift cards and Internet shopping, fewer people are giving gifts of homemade food. Perhaps that is why such presents are so treasured. Here are some simple packaging tips to accompany easy recipes from this book.

———

I prefer wrappings that showcase the food, such as glass jars, cellophane bags, replicas of vintage tin plates, or plain tins lined with waxed paper. Large stores that specialize in containers and wrappings are good places to find decorative waxed paper, rolls of cellophane, and glass jars of various sizes. Have ribbon or natural raffia on hand, and for a final touch, tuck in a sprig of fresh rosemary or holly leaves. While you're in the kitchen, make several batches ahead for multiple gifts—and keep some for yourself for entertaining over the holidays.

MUGS OF HOT CHOCOLATE, PAGE 46
A wonderful gift for teachers or families with young kids.

Purchase a large, latte-style mug. Mix together the cocoa powder, salt, and bittersweet chocolate (double the amounts for a generous gift), and spoon into a small cellophane bag. Tie with a ribbon, attaching a copy of the recipe on a tag (so the recipient knows how to proceed), and place inside the mug.

VARIATIONS:
Tie a candy cane or a bundle of cinnamon sticks to the ribbon for swirling into the hot chocolate.

Include a small immersion milk frother, available from kitchen supply stores or online, for making a sophisticated version of the recipe.

SERIOUSLY SIMPLE SEASONING SALT, PAGE 208
Purchase small glass containers topped with shakers. Mix together the seasoning salt and transfer to the containers. Store any remaining salt in an airtight container. Before screwing on the shaker tops, cover the containers with plastic wrap. This will allow the salt to last for several months, refrigerated. Attach a label to the container and tie raffia around the top.

CRANBERRY POMEGRANATE SAUCE WITH SATSUMAS, PAGE 212

Ideal as a Thanksgiving hostess gift or around Christmas. The sauce needs to stay refrigerated and eaten within a week.

Purchase glass jars with clamp lids. Prepare a batch of sauce and pour into several small jars or one large jar. Tie a red or orange satin ribbon around each jar, along with a tag.

SPICY SAUSAGE AND CHICKEN LIVER PÂTÉ, PAGE 52

Prepare the recipe using small ceramic crocks. When the crocks are fully chilled, wrap each in cellophane, gathering it at the top and securing it with raffia. Slip a sprig of fresh rosemary under the raffia. Indicate on the tag that the pâté should be kept refrigerated and eaten within five days.

BALSAMIC GLAZE, PAGE 209

Purchase tall glass vinegar cruets and add the vinegar once it has cooled. Seal tightly and refrigerate. Add a ribbon and tag indicating that the vinegar may be kept for up to three months, refrigerated.

MAPLE-PEAR APPLESAUCE, PAGE 214

Another gift that lends itself well to the fall holidays, especially for families with young children. Prepare a batch of applesauce and spoon into glass jars with clamp lids. Attach a label telling the recipient that the applesauce keeps for 1 week in the refrigerator, and tie raffia around the top.

DRIED FRUIT AND CHOCOLATE BAR COOKIES, PAGE 197

Place the bars in an airtight cookie tin. Wrap with cellophane and ribbon.

MENUS

ROSH HASHANAH
(MAY NEED ADJUSTMENT FOR THOSE KEEPING KOSHER)

CHILLED WHITEFISH AND SALMON TERRINE WITH HERBED HORSERADISH CREAM (page 164)

BRISKET WITH FIGS AND BUTTERNUT SQUASH (page 130)

GREEN BEANS WITH CARAMELIZED RED ONION AND MUSHROOM TOPPING (page 180)

NOODLE KUGEL (page 174) *or* ROASTED POTATO WEDGES WITH LEEKS AND THYME (page 184)

DRIED FRUIT COMPOTE WITH HONEY MASCARPONE (page 192)

PURCHASED BISCOTTI

———

KOL NIDRE
(MAY NEED ADJUSTMENT FOR THOSE KEEPING KOSHER)

CHICKEN-VEGETABLE SOUP WITH HERBED MATZO BALLS (page 73)

PLUM-GLAZED TURKEY BREAST WITH SAKE AND PEAR SAUCE (page 119)

RICE PILAF WITH DRIED CHERRIES AND TOASTED PISTACHIOS (page 189)

CHOCOLATE-DRIED CHERRY BREAD PUDDING (page 202)

———

SUNDAY SUPPER

BABY GREENS WITH AUTUMN FRUIT AND WARM GOAT CHEESE (page 77)

GREEN LENTIL SOUP WITH SAUSAGES AND RED PEPPERS (page 75)

WARM ASSORTED ROLLS

BREAKFAST CROSTINI (page 96)

———

EARLY FALL LAST-MINUTE DINNER

LIME-MINT SLAW (page 83)

SLOW-ROASTED SALMON WITH MISO VINAIGRETTE (page 151)

STEAMED BROCCOLI

APPLE CLAFOUTI (page 200)

———

HALLOWEEN

HOT MULLED CIDER (page 47) (nonalcoholic)

CRUDITÉS WITH ASSORTED STORE-BOUGHT DIPS SUCH AS ARTICHOKE, SPINACH, AND YOGURT AND CUCUMBER

BAKED PASTA WITH TOMATO, RED PEPPER, AND SWEET ITALIAN SAUSAGE SAUCE (page 169)

SIMPLE GREEN SALAD

SOUR CREAM-VANILLA CUPCAKES (page 198) (let the kids decorate them)

———

THANKSGIVING FOR A CROWD

SPICY SAUSAGE AND CHICKEN LIVER PÂTÉ (page 52)

ROAST TURKEY WITH MAPLE-BALSAMIC BUTTER RUB (page 112) AND MAKE-AHEAD TURKEY GRAVY (page 216)

continued on next page

THANKSGIVING FOR A CROWD (CONTINUED)

CORNBREAD, OYSTER, AND RED PEPPER STUFFING
(page 186)

CRANBERRY-POMEGRANATE SAUCE WITH
SATSUMAS (page 212) *or* ORANGE-CRANBERRY
SAUCE (page 213)

PERFECT MASHED POTATOES (page 185)

YAM AND WINTER SQUASH PURÉE (page 178)

GREEN BEANS WITH CARAMELIZED RED
ONION AND MUSHROOM TOPPING (page 180)

PUMPKIN-CARAMEL ICE CREAM PIE (page 195)
WITH WARM CARAMEL SAUCE (page 218)

DOUBLE-PERSIMMON PUDDING (page 193)

========

AN INTIMATE THANKSGIVING DINNER

PERSIMMON AND WINTER SQUASH SOUP
WITH LEMON-NUTMEG CREAM (page 68)

TURKEY WITH ORANGE-HERB BASTING SAUCE
(page 121) *or* CORNISH HENS WITH BRAISED
CABBAGE AND APPLE (page 110)

PERFECT MASHED POTATOES (page 185)

ROASTED BRUSSELS SPROUTS (page 177)

CRANBERRY AND PEAR CUSTARD CRISP (page 196)

========

RELAXING HOLIDAY LUNCH FOR FRIENDS

FENNEL, POTATO, AND CARROT SOUP (page 70)

WINTER CHOPPED SALAD (page 80)

ASSORTED BREADS AND OLIVE OILS

APPLE CLAFOUTI (page 200)

HANUKKAH

MEDITERRANEAN-STYLE CHICKEN WITH
CAPERS, PLUMS, AND OLIVES
(page 107)

POTATO PANCAKE FRITTATA (page 183)

MAPLE-PEAR APPLESAUCE (page 214)

SUGAR COOKIES *or* SOUR CREAM–VANILLA
CUPCAKES (page 198)

========

EASY FAMILY CHRISTMAS EVE

MIXED GREENS WITH PERSIMMONS, PROSCIUTTO,
AND SHAVED PARMESAN (page 82)

CIOPPINO (page 160)

ASSORTED BREADS, CHEESES, AND FRUIT

CHOCOLATE–DRIED CHERRY BREAD PUDDING
(page 202)

========

INTIMATE CHRISTMAS EVE

TWO-ENDIVE SALAD WITH PEAR, WALNUTS,
AND BLUE CHEESE (page 79)

ROAST DUCK LEGS WITH CARAMELIZED
SHALLOTS AND GARLIC (page 127)

POLENTA WITH BUTTERNUT SQUASH
AND CHESTNUTS (page 182)

CRANBERRY AND PEAR CUSTARD CRISP
(page 196)

CHRISTMAS BREAKFAST

CRANBERRY MIMOSA (page 49)

PANETTONE BREAKFAST PUDDING WITH
EGGNOG CUSTARD (page 88)
or SAVORY BREAD PUDDING WITH BACON,
PEPPERS, AND SPINACH (page 90)

WINTER FRUIT PLATTER

CHOCOLATE-CHIP PECAN CRUMB COFFEE CAKE
(page 94)

———

VEGETARIAN HOLIDAY DINNER

BAKED BRIE WITH TOASTED ALMONDS AND
CRANBERRY GLAZE (page 60)

BABY GREENS WITH AUTUMN FRUIT (page 77)
(omit the cheese)

POLENTA WITH BUTTERNUT SQUASH AND
CHESTNUTS (page 182) *or* BUTTERNUT SQUASH
LASAGNA (page 172)

ROASTED BRUSSELS SPROUTS
(page 177)

CHOCOLATE-TOFFEE PIE
(page 201)

———

CHRISTMAS DINNER

POTATO PANCAKE FRITTATA (page 183)
WITH SMOKED SALMON, CRÈME FRAÎCHE,
AND CAVIAR

TWO-ENDIVE SALAD WITH PEAR,
WALNUTS, AND BLUE CHEESE
(page 79)

STANDING RIB ROAST WITH HORSERADISH
CREAM AND CABERNET SAUCE (page 134)

BRAISED SPINACH WITH CRISPY SHALLOTS
(page 175)

CHOCOLATE-PEPPERMINT PUDDING CAKES WITH
PEPPERMINT STICK ICE CREAM (page 205)

———

COCKTAIL PARTY FOR A CROWD

CRUDITÉS PLATTER FROM THE MARKET WITH
ASSORTED DIPS

SPICY SAUSAGE AND CHICKEN LIVER PÂTÉ
(page 52) WITH CRACKERS

TOMATO-OLIVE TOASTS (page 57)

BAKED BRIE WITH TOASTED ALMONDS AND
CRANBERRY GLAZE (page 60)

CRISPY BACON-WRAPPED STUFFED DATES
(page 59)

CITRUS-MARINATED SEAFOOD (page 55)

PERSIMMONS WRAPPED IN PROSCIUTTO (page 63)

ASSORTED WINES AND SPARKLING WINES

———

NEW YEAR'S EVE SUPPER

OLIVE OIL AND SLICED FRENCH BREAD

BABY GREENS WITH AUTUMN FRUIT AND
WARM GOAT CHEESE (page 77)

NEW YEAR'S EVE ONION SOUP WITH
PARMESAN-GRUYÈRE CROUTONS (page 71)

DRIED FRUIT AND CHOCOLATE BAR COOKIES
(page 197)

NEW YEAR'S EVE DINNER FOR FOUR

CRISPY BACON-WRAPPED STUFFED DATES
(page 59)

MUSHROOM AND POTATO BISQUE WITH
PANCETTA CROUTONS (page 66)

BLACK PEPPER STEAK (page 132)

BRAISED SPINACH WITH CRISPY SHALLOTS
(page 175)

ROASTED POTATO WEDGES WITH
LEEKS AND THYME (page 184)

CHOCOLATE-PEPPERMINT PUDDING CAKES WITH
PEPPERMINT STICK ICE CREAM
(page 205)

=====

WINTER GET-GOING BREAKFAST

CITRUS POPOVER PANCAKE WITH
MASCARPONE AND BERRIES (page 93)

CRISP BACON

ORANGE AND GRAPEFRUIT JUICES MIXED WITH
POMEGRANATE JUICE

=====

HOLIDAY BRUNCH

POMEGRANATE CHAMPAGNE COCKTAIL
(page 48)

SCRAMBLED EGGS WITH CARAMELIZED
ONIONS, SMOKED SALMON, AND HERBED CREAM
CHEESE (page 97)

CHOCOLATE-CHIP PECAN CRUMB COFFEE
CAKE (page 94) *or* TOASTED BAGELS WITH
ASSORTED JAMS

PITCHERS OF ASSORTED JUICES

PLATE OF SLICED WINTER FRUIT

=====

EASY NEW YEAR'S DAY

WHITE WINE FRUIT SPRITZER (page 49)

GREEN SALAD WITH BASIC VINAIGRETTE AND
SLICED VEGETABLES

PINEAPPLE-HONEY-GLAZED HAM (page 144)

FAVORITE POTATO SALAD

LIME-MINT SLAW (page 83)

CHOCOLATE-TOFFEE PIE (page 201)

=====

FOOTBALL NEW YEAR'S DAY

HOLIDAY SEAFOOD GUMBO (page 157), WITH SLICED
FRENCH BREAD OR ROLLS
or TURKEY AND PINTO BEAN CHILI (page 124),
WITH ASSORTED SALSAS, GRATED CHEDDAR
CHEESE, AND SOUR CREAM *and*
SPICY JALAPEÑO CORNBREAD (page 100)

SLICED WINTER FRUIT PLATE

DRIED FRUIT AND CHOCOLATE BAR COOKIES
(page 197)

Pairing Holiday Wine and Cheese

BY PETER MARKS

Most of us believe wine and cheese are natural partners that enhance the quality and flavors of each other. This is often true, but the tremendous diversity of wines and cheeses makes each situation unique.

———

That said, there are some simple guidelines you can follow when planning your holiday entertaining. Most cheeses can be grouped into one of five major categories. From there it's easy to select an accompanying wine.

BLUE CHEESES:

The moldy flavors of blue cheeses often fight with dry wines and can be tough on reds. Sweet wines are perfect partners, such as Sauternes with Roquefort or port with Stilton. Late-harvest whites such as Chenin Blanc, Pinot Gris, Riesling, and Semillon are usually a match made in heaven.

EXTREME CHEESES:

Cheeses with bizarre and loud personalities include Époisses, Munster, and Limburger. Some of these cheeses are spiced or smoked. As fun as these cheeses can be, usually only sweet or fortified wines can hold their own against them. Consider a sweet sherry, Madeira, Sauternes, Hungarian Tokaji, or late-harvest Gewürztraminer.

GOAT AND SHEEP CHEESES:

Cheeses fit into this category when the tangy flavor of the milk predominates. Young goat-milk cheeses cry out for a crisp young white such as Sauvignon Blanc, Pinot Gris, Chenin Blanc, or French Chablis. Harder, more mature cheeses such as pecorino have an affinity for lively reds such as Sangiovese or Zinfandel.

HARD CHEESES:

These cheeses match with a greater range of wines than those of any other category. Their firm consistency does not leave a trail of mouth-coating butterfat. Their deeper, more mature flavors can work well with powerful and complex reds, especially mature Cabernet Sauvignon, Merlot, Syrah, Italian Barolo, and Spanish Rioja, and even whites with some bottle age.

SOFT CHEESES:

The mouth-coating texture of soft cheeses can make red wines taste thin and tough. The effervescence of Champagne and sparkling wines cuts through beautifully. A crisp aromatic white (Riesling, for instance) can also do well, especially if it has a bit of sweetness.

The Cheese Course: First and Last

Following are ideas for cheese courses to pair with wine, using the
wine selection guidelines on the previous page. The starter course could be
served before a meal or as an appetizer as guests are arriving. The last course
offers suggestions for a dessert spread to serve after dinner,
or even as a late-night course on its own.

―――――――――

Cheese courses are the essence of Seriously Simple; they are easy to assemble, elegant, and flavorful. Choose three or four different cheeses with a variety of textures, such as soft, semisoft, and firm. Pair the cheeses with sliced bread, crackers, fresh fruit, and high-end condiments or nuts, depending upon the course served. Remove the cheeses from the refrigerator at least 30 minutes before serving, keeping them wrapped. They should be eaten at slightly below room temperature. Just before serving, arrange wedges of cheese on a large wooden tray, flat wicker basket, or flat ceramic platter, grouping the fruits, nuts, breads, or condiments around the cheeses. To prepare the platter ahead, cover just the cheeses with plastic wrap or a damp kitchen towel, and add the accompaniments before serving.

STARTER COURSE

These are highly flavorful cheeses with nutty flavors. Look for goat cheese logs coated with herbs or seasonings. Add a country pâté or slices of smoked salmon for a heartier platter.

DRY JACK
CHÈVRE
PORT-SALUT OR MORBIER
GRUYÈRE OR COMTÉ
―――――
APPLES (FUJI OR PINK LADY), THINLY SLICED
GRAPES, IN CLUSTERS
―――――
FRESH BAGUETTE, SLICED
WATER CRACKERS

CONDIMENTS:

OLIVES, CHUTNEY, HONEY MUSTARD

ADDITIONS:

PÂTÉS, SMOKED SALMON

DRIED FRUIT AND NUTS:

DRIED PEARS, ALMONDS, PECANS, PISTACHIOS

DESSERT COURSE

The colors and flavors of British cheeses, such as sharp, nutty Cheddars and smooth, blue-veined Stiltons, fit well with autumn. Pair these with a creamy, mild Camembert for a well-balanced platter. Small local farms produce their own artisan cheeses, such as Point Reyes blue, so look for their counterparts in specialty shops with good cheese counters.

PEARS (ASIAN OR RED BARTLETT), THINLY SLICED
GRAPES (RED OR GREEN), IN SMALL CLUSTERS

BLUE STILTON
FARMHOUSE CHEDDAR
CAMEMBERT
TRIPLE CREAM LIKE SAINT-ANDRÉ

COUNTRY BREAD (WHOLE GRAIN, OR WITH NUTS OR DRIED FRUIT), SLICED
ENGLISH TABLE WATER CRACKERS

CONDIMENTS:

FIG COMPOTE, KUMQUAT MARMALADE, WHITE TRUFFLE HONEY

DRIED FRUIT AND NUTS:

SPANISH ALMONDS, DRIED APRICOTS, FIGS, OR DATES

SEASONAL DRINKS

HOT CHOCOLATE

Fred Thompson, author of *Hot Chocolate*, might just be the king of hot chocolate. This is his grown-up rendition of American hot chocolate. Until recently, most Americans have preferred a sweeter hot chocolate than is customarily served in Europe and South America. This version incorporates a little more sweetness, as well as creaminess, while holding on to a bit of European character. If you want to splurge on an immersion milk frother, you can finish with some frothy steamed milk.

INGREDIENTS:

4 TABLESPOONS SWEETENED COCOA POWDER

2½ OUNCES BITTERSWEET CHOCO-LATE (70 TO 75 PERCENT CACAO), CHOPPED

LARGE PINCH KOSHER SALT

4 CUPS MILK

GRATED BITTERSWEET CHOCOLATE FOR GARNISH (OPTIONAL)

In a medium, heavy saucepan, combine the cocoa, chopped chocolate, salt, and milk. Place over medium heat and whisk gently. When the chocolate melts and the cocoa dissolves, raise the heat to medium-high and whisk more vigorously to form froth on the surface. When the mixture bubbles around the edges and seems ready to boil, remove from the heat. Do not let it boil. Ladle into 4 small cups, including some froth on each. Garnish with grated chocolate, if desired. Serve immediately.

ADVANCE PREPARATION:

Mix together the cocoa powder, chopped chocolate, and salt and store in an airtight container for up to 1 month in a cool, dark place.

THE CLEVER COOK COULD:

◦ Garnish the servings with dollops of chocolate whipped cream. Whisk ½ cup chilled heavy cream with 1 teaspoon sweetened cocoa powder until peaks form.

◦ Add a drop or more of peppermint extract to the milk mixture after the chocolate has melted.

◦ Double the recipe by using a 3-quart saucepan.

HOT MULLED CIDER

My friend Laurie Burrows Grad makes this warming cider each year for her big holiday party. She likes it better than mulled wine, because if it spills, it won't stain the carpet. The cider is very easy to prepare and economical to serve for a crowd. You can also halve the recipe for a smaller group. I like to ladle it right from my stove so it stays warm. You can also put the cider in a container on a hot plate if you need to keep the kitchen clear. For a children's Halloween party, omit the rum. Packets of mulling spices are sold in supermarkets and gourmet stores.

INGREDIENTS:

¼ CUP MULLING SPICES

1 ORANGE, SLICED CROSSWISE

1 LEMON, SLICED CROSSWISE

1 GALLON STORE-BOUGHT APPLE CIDER, FRESHLY PRESSED PREFERRED

½ TO 1 CUP LIGHT RUM

CINNAMON STICKS FOR GARNISH

1. Combine the mulling spices and fruit in a cheesecloth bag, and tie the bag securely with kitchen twine. (Or use a couple of mulling spice bags and add the fruit slices to the cider.)

2. In a large nonaluminum stock pot, combine the bag of spices and fruit and the cider. Bring to a boil over high heat, reduce the heat to low, and simmer for about 45 minutes. Remove the bag, squeezing the essence of the spices into the cider, and discard the bag.

3. About 10 to 15 minutes before serving, stir in the rum and allow the mixture to heat through. Do not boil.

4. Serve the mulled cider warm in cups with handles, accompanied by cinnamon stick stirrers.

ADVANCE PREPARATION:
Make through step 2 up to 2 days ahead, cover, and refrigerate until ready to heat with the rum.

POMEGRANATE CHAMPAGNE COCKTAIL

❧ SERVES 6 ❧

This is a festive way to begin a special brunch or dinner. I like to serve this with Crispy Bacon-Wrapped Stuffed Dates (page 59).

INGREDIENTS:

6 TABLESPOONS POMEGRANATE JUICE

2 TABLESPOONS POMEGRANATE SEEDS

ONE 750-ML BOTTLE CHAMPAGNE OR SPARKLING WINE, CHILLED

Pour 1 tablespoon of the pomegranate juice into each Champagne flute. Add a few pomegranate seeds (they will drop to the bottom). Pour about 4 ounces of Champagne into each flute. Serve immediately.

BLOODY MARY

❧ SERVES 12 ❧

Set out a large pitcher of the tomato base so it is ready for guests. This is great for a brunch or New Year's Day. For those who prefer a nonalcoholic version, pour the base over ice and garnish with a celery stick.

INGREDIENTS:

BASE

ONE 46-OUNCE CAN TOMATO JUICE

½ CUP FRESH LEMON OR LIME JUICE

¼ CUP WORCESTERSHIRE SAUCE

TABASCO SAUCE TO TASTE

SALT AND FRESHLY CRACKED BLACK PEPPER TO TASTE

ICE CUBES

ONE 750-ML BOTTLE VODKA, CHILLED

12 CELERY STICKS WITH LEAVES FOR GARNISH

1. Make the base: In a large pitcher, combine all of the ingredients. Stir to blend.

2. Add ice cubes and 1 to 2 ounces of vodka to each glass. Pour in the base. Garnish with a celery stick and serve.

ADVANCE PREPARATION:
Make up to 1 day ahead through step 1, cover, and refrigerate.

WHITE WINE FRUIT SPRITZER

This refreshing, colorful drink, a light version of sangría, will delight your guests. I like to serve the spritzer at a cocktail party or as a welcoming beverage at brunch. For the white wine, my favorite choice is Viognier. Be sure to make the spritzers just before serving.

INGREDIENTS:

ONE 750-ML BOTTLE WHITE WINE, CHILLED

3 CUPS SPARKLING WATER, CHILLED

1½ CUPS TANGERINE JUICE, CHILLED

1½ CUPS CRANBERRY JUICE, CHILLED

8 TO 10 MINT LEAVES, CRUSHED

1½ CUPS CRUSHED ICE

1 ORANGE, SLICED CROSSWISE

1 TANGERINE, SLICED CROSSWISE

1 CUP FROZEN STRAWBERRIES

In a large glass pitcher, combine all of the liquid ingredients. Add the mint, crushed ice, and fruit. Stir to combine with a long spoon. Pour into pretty goblets and serve.

THE CLEVER COOK COULD:
- Use Sauvignon Blanc, Fumé Blanc, or California Rosé.
- Substitute guava, pomegranate, pineapple, or other juices for the tangerine and cranberry.

CRANBERRY MIMOSA

This version of the classic mimosa uses cranberry instead of orange juice. Serve this as a festive beginning to a holiday brunch.

INGREDIENTS:

18 FRESH CRANBERRIES, WASHED AND PICKED OVER

¾ CUP CRANBERRY JUICE, CHILLED

ONE 750-ML BOTTLE CHAMPAGNE OR SPARKLING WINE, CHILLED

Place 3 cranberries in each Champagne flute. Pour 2 tablespoons of the cranberry juice into each flute. Pour in the Champagne so each flute is about three-quarters full. Serve immediately.

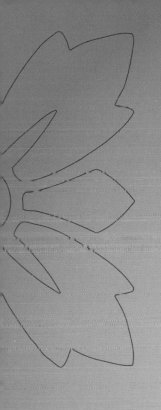

APPETIZERS

SPICY SAUSAGE AND CHICKEN LIVER PÂTÉ

❊ SERVES 12 TO 18 ❊

Want a showstopper for a crowd? Try this appetizer, which has been my signature at holiday parties for as long as I can remember. What is so great about this pâté is that you can make it up to a month ahead and freeze it. In addition, kids love it as much as adults do. For a large party, mold the pâté in an 8-inch springform pan. Shortly before serving, carefully release the sides of the pan. You can also use ramekins of various capacities and freeze them for different-size gatherings. If you are unable to find spicy pork sausage, add red pepper flakes to taste when you mix in the spices in step 3.

INGREDIENTS:

¼ CUP DRIED CURRANTS

½ CUP APPLE BRANDY

4 TABLESPOONS UNSALTED BUTTER

4 TABLESPOONS OLIVE OIL

2 ONIONS, FINELY CHOPPED

2 PIPPIN APPLES, PEELED, CORED, AND FINELY CHOPPED

3 GARLIC CLOVES, MINCED

2½ TEASPOONS SALT

½ TEASPOON DRIED THYME

¼ TEASPOON GROUND ALLSPICE

¼ TEASPOON GROUND WHITE PEPPER

1 POUND CREAM CHEESE, SOFTENED AND CUT INTO 2-INCH PIECES

1 POUND SPICY PORK SAUSAGE

1 POUND CHICKEN LIVERS, CLEANED AND RINSED

¼ CUP COARSELY CHOPPED UNSALTED RAW PISTACHIOS, PLUS WHOLE PISTACHIOS FOR GARNISH

PARSLEY SPRIGS FOR GARNISH

1. Place the currants in a small saucepan and pour the apple brandy over them. Bring to a boil over medium-high heat. Remove from the heat and let currants steep for at least 30 minutes, or until softened.

2. In a large skillet, melt 3 tablespoons of the butter with 2 tablespoons of the oil over medium heat. Sauté the onions for about 5 minutes, or until softened. Add the apples and cook for 3 to 5 minutes, or until nicely softened. Add the garlic and cook for 1 minute.

3. Transfer the mixture to a food processor fitted with the metal blade and purée. Add the salt, thyme, allspice, white pepper, and cream cheese and process until puréed.

4. In the same skillet, melt the remaining 1 tablespoon butter with the remaining 2 tablespoons oil over medium-high heat. Cook the sausage, stirring, for about 5 minutes, or until evenly browned. Add the chicken livers and sauté until cooked through and no pinkness remains. Drain the fat. Drain

the currants, reserving the brandy, and add the brandy to the skillet. Remove the skillet from the heat and make sure that the overhead fan is not on. Ignite the brandy with a long match, averting your head.

5. When the flame has gone out, add the liver mixture to the onion-apple mixture in the food processor and process for about 30 seconds, or until smooth. Add the softened currants and chopped pistachios and process until just

combined, making sure that the currants and pistachios retain their texture. Taste and adjust the seasonings.

6. Pour into two 4-cup crocks or molds. Decorate with the whole pistachios and garnish with the parsley. Chill for at least 4 hours before serving.

ADVANCE PREPARATION:
Make up to 5 days ahead, cover, and refrigerate. Freeze up to 1 month ahead (without the garnish).

THE CLEVER COOK COULD:
- Mold the pâté in a springform pan. After releasing the sides, decorate the top of the pâté with cherry tomato quarters arranged as flower petals, a chive stem, and a border of fresh dill.
- Unmold the pâté from the springform pan onto a large round platter, cover the sides with finely chopped fresh parsley, and surround with simple water crackers and thinly sliced French bread.

CITRUS-MARINATED SEAFOOD

This colorful, tangy appetizer is a refreshing change from the traditional shrimp cocktail. I like to combine the briny shrimp with bay scallops, the tiny, sweet variety. Watch carefully when cooking the seafood—it can overcook quickly, resulting in a rubbery consistency. If you are serving this dish with cocktails, put out some pretty toothpicks for spearing. The seafood can also be offered as a first course. For convenience, and to save time, ask your fishmonger to peel and devein the shrimp for you.

INGREDIENTS:

MARINADE

¾ CUP FRESH LEMON JUICE

1¼ CUPS OLIVE OIL

2 GARLIC CLOVES, MINCED

1 TABLESPOON DIJON MUSTARD

PINCH RED PEPPER FLAKES

SALT AND FRESHLY GROUND BLACK PEPPER TO TASTE

———

2 CUPS WATER

2 CUPS DRY WHITE WINE SUCH AS SAUVIGNON BLANC OR PINOT GRIS

1 BAY LEAF

1½ POUNDS MEDIUM SHRIMP (APPROXIMATELY 30 PER POUND), PEELED AND DEVEINED

1½ POUNDS BAY SCALLOPS

1 RED BELL PEPPER, SEEDED, THINLY SLICED, AND CUT INTO 2-INCH LENGTHS

1 YELLOW BELL PEPPER, SEEDED, THINLY SLICED, AND CUT INTO 2-INCH LENGTHS

1 RED ONION, HALVED AND THINLY SLICED

½ CUP KALAMATA OLIVES, PITTED AND COARSELY CHOPPED

1 LEMON (MEYER, IF POSSIBLE), HALVED AND THINLY SLICED

¼ CUP FINELY CHOPPED FRESH PARSLEY

RED LEAF LETTUCE FOR SERVING

1. Make the marinade: Place all the ingredients in a medium nonaluminum bowl. Whisk just until combined. Taste and adjust the seasonings.

2. In a large saucepan, combine the water, wine, and bay leaf over medium-high heat. Bring to a boil. Add the shrimp, cover, and cook, stirring occasionally, for 3 to 4 minutes, or until the shrimp are pink on the outside and just cooked in the center. Using a slotted spoon, remove to a deep bowl or large rectangular plastic container. Return the cooking liquid to a boil, add the scallops, and cook for 2 to 3 minutes, or until the center of each scallop is opaque. Remove with the slotted spoon and add to the shrimp.

3. Add the red and yellow bell peppers, onion, olives, lemon, and parsley to the seafood. Pour in the marinade and stir well to combine the ingredients and coat the seafood. Refrigerate for at least 4 hours

continued on next page

. . . continued

or up to overnight, stirring the seafood occasionally to marinate evenly.

4. To serve, arrange the lettuce on a large platter and, using a slotted spoon, top with the seafood mixture. Drizzle a little of the marinade over the seafood. Serve with small plates and forks or toothpicks, or serve on individual plates as a first course.

ADVANCE PREPARATION:
Make up to 1 day ahead through step 3, cover, and refrigerate. Remove from the refrigerator 15 minutes before serving.

THE CLEVER COOK COULD:
- Spoon the seafood mixture onto endive leaves rather than lettuce.
- Serve the seafood mixture as a luncheon buffet dish along with other salads.
- Present the mixture in a glass bowl set in a larger bowl of crushed ice.
- Serve dollops of the mixture on crostini.

TOMATO-OLIVE TOASTS

Sun-dried tomato pesto gives these toasts an intense flavor and serves as a base for a touch of olive tapenade and Parmesan cheese. Using prepared pesto and tapenade, sold at supermarkets and gourmet stores, guarantees that this appetizer is easy to put together. Sample the available varieties and choose your favorite.

INGREDIENTS:

24 THIN SLICES FRENCH OR SOUR-DOUGH BREAD, BAGUETTE STYLE (ABOUT 2½-INCHES IN DIAMETER)

2 TABLESPOONS PLUS 1 TEASPOON OLIVE OIL

¼ CUP SUN-DRIED TOMATO PESTO

2 TABLESPOONS TAPENADE

3 TABLESPOONS FRESHLY GRATED PARMESAN CHEESE

1. Preheat the oven to 375°F. Place the bread slices on a baking sheet and toast them for 5 minutes, or until dry and firm but not golden. Let cool.

2. In a small bowl, combine the olive oil and pesto. Stir to mix well. Brush each toast with the pesto mixture. Top with a tiny spoonful of the tapenade and then sprinkle evenly with the Parmesan. Arrange the toasts on the baking sheet.

3. Bake for about 5 minutes, or until the cheese is melted but not browned. Watch carefully to avoid burning. Let cool before serving.

ADVANCE PREPARATION:
Make the toasts up to 3 days ahead and store in an airtight container at room temperature.

THE CLEVER COOK COULD:
° Serve the toasts in a basket to accompany soups or salads.
° Use the toasts as a garnish for soups or salads.

CRISPY BACON-WRAPPED STUFFED DATES

❊ SERVES 6 TO 8 ❊

Sounds a bit like a twist on rumaki? I first tasted this classic Spanish appetizer at a wonderful restaurant in Los Angeles, called AOC, that specializes in tapas. At once sweet, smoky, and salty, the little brown nuggets are a crowd pleaser, the perfect pick-up nibble to offer with cocktails. To make small shards of Parmesan cheese, cut them from a wedge of cheese with a sharp knife. Serve the dates hot from the oven while the cheese is still warm and watch how fast they disappear.

INGREDIENTS:

18 LARGE MEDJOOL DATES

18 PIECES PARMESAN CHEESE, EACH ABOUT 1 INCH BY ¼ INCH

6 SLICES APPLE-CURED BACON, EACH CUT INTO THIRDS

1 BUNCH PARSLEY, STEMS REMOVED, FOR GARNISH

1. Preheat the oven to 450°F. Slit each date along one side and carefully remove the pit. Insert a piece of Parmesan into each slit. Wrap a piece of bacon around each stuffed date and secure with a toothpick. Place the dates on a baking sheet.

2. Bake for about 5 minutes, or until the bacon on top is crisp. Using tongs, turn the dates and bake for another 5 minutes, or until the bacon is crisp. Transfer the dates to a double layer of paper towels to drain.

3. Place the parsley bunch in the center of a round serving platter and arrange the dates around the parsley. Serve immediately.

ADVANCE PREPARATION:
Make up to 1 day ahead through step 1, cover, and refrigerate. Bring to room temperature before baking.

THE CLEVER COOK COULD:
- Arrange the dates on top of mixed greens dressed with Basic Vinaigrette (page 210) for an unusual first course.
- Substitute different cheeses such as dry Sonoma Jack or Pecorino Toscano.

BAKED BRIE WITH TOASTED ALMONDS AND CRANBERRY GLAZE

❄ SERVES 4 TO 6 ❄

This holiday taste teaser is always a big hit. For a cocktail party, I sometimes make a few rounds using different glazes and place them around the house. Make sure to serve the Brie hot from the oven, when the cheese is warm, creamy, and at its best.

INGREDIENTS:

ONE 8-OUNCE ROUND BRIE, CHILLED

3 TABLESPOONS ORANGE-CRANBERRY SAUCE (PAGE 213) OR STORE-BOUGHT CHUTNEY

3 TABLESPOONS TOASTED SLIVERED ALMONDS

WATER CRACKERS OR THINLY SLICED FRENCH BREAD

1. Preheat the oven to 325°F.

2. Scrape the rind off the top of the Brie with a sharp knife. Cut the Brie in half horizontally so you have 2 circles. Place the bottom circle on an ovenproof glass plate. Top with 2 tablespoons of the cranberry sauce and spread evenly. Sprinkle evenly with 1 tablespoon of the almonds. Top with the remaining circle and spread with the remaining 1 tablespoon cranberry sauce. Sprinkle with the remaining 2 tablespoons almonds.

3. Bake for about 7 minutes, or until the Brie is very soft but not melted. Place on a trivet to serve. Accompany with the water crackers.

ADVANCE PREPARATION:
Make up to 6 hours ahead through step 2, cover, and refrigerate. Remove from the refrigerator 30 minutes before baking.

_____

THE CLEVER COOK COULD:
- Use a 1 pound Brie to serve a larger crowd. Double the quantities of sauce or chutney and nuts, and bake for a few minutes longer, or until soft and warm.
- Try different combinations— apricot jam and almonds; dates and walnuts; fig jam and pecans.
- Make a jam by cooking mixed dried fruits, port wine, and a little brown sugar until the fruits are soft. Use the jam with your favorite mixed nuts.

_____

APPETIZERS FROM THE MARKET TO THE TABLE

———

Take advantage of the growing number of specialty foods available in markets, to serve on their own or to use as a great starting point for building your own appetizers. Keep your pantry stocked with a variety of useful items that can be transformed into quick starters. This can help save you a lot of time.

NO-TIME APPETIZERS

* Candied pecans or walnuts. Look for glazed or chili-spiced nuts and serve them with cocktails.
* Spanish Marcona almonds.
* Roasted pumpkin seeds.
* Edamame, roasted and shelled or in the shell, sprinkled with kosher salt.
* Hummus and yogurt-cucumber, blue cheese, eggplant, and other prepared dips, added to a platter of raw vegetables.
* Onion- or other flavored crackers topped with smoked salmon and cream cheese dip, caramelized onions, or kalamata olives and feta cheese.
* Mini toasts topped with different store-bought pestos, tapenades, and vegetable spreads.
* Olive bar. In small glass bowls, put together a colorful variety of different olives from around the world, including store-bought stuffed olives filled with blue cheese, garlic, or roasted peppers.

———

SLIGHT ASSEMBLY REQUIRED

* Antipasto platter. Suggested items available at Italian delis include roasted peppers, small balls of mozzarella called *bocconcini* or *perlini*, mushrooms, olives, and artichoke hearts.

Purchase these ingredients already marinated, or marinate them in Basic Vinaigrette (page 210). Include sliced salami or mortadella on the platter. Arrange the ingredients in long rows and serve with flat bread, focaccia, or bread sticks.

- Belgian endive leaves filled with smoked salmon and crème fraîche, sour cream and salsa, or a mixture of blue cheese and cream cheese topped with bay shrimp.

- Smoked salmon or gravlax thinly sliced and surrounded on a platter with pumpernickel toasts and honey Dijon mustard, or served on a platter with capers, lemon wedges, and buttered thin toasts.

- Pasta Frittata (page 99) or Potato Pancake Frittata (page 183), or a variation, cut into bite-size pieces.

- Toasted baguette slices topped with a slice of Brie cheese, a thin slice of prosciutto, and a dollop of fig compote.

- Fuyu persimmons, peeled and cut into 2-inch slices, wrapped in thin slices of serrano ham or prosciutto, secured with a skewer, and drizzled with Balsamic Glaze (page 209).

- Fresh figs, quartered, topped with softened sweet Gorgonzola cheese, and drizzled with Balsamic Glaze (page 209).

- One 6-ounce can tuna packed in oil puréed with 1 tablespoon each olive oil, sun-dried tomato pesto, and capers. Add 1 teaspoon Balsamic Glaze (page 209) and season with fresh herbs. Serve on crackers or cucumber slices.

- Ricotta cheese blended with store-bought eggplant spread and sun-dried tomato pesto. Serve with crackers.

SOUPS AND SALADS

MUSHROOM AND POTATO BISQUE WITH PANCETTA CROUTONS

SERVES 6 TO 8

Dried mushrooms combined with fresh cremini give the bisque a particularly rich mushroom flavor. The pancetta "croutons" are a natural companion to the earthy mushrooms and add a crispy texture to the creamy soup. The soy sauce brings out the mushroom flavor. Serve the bisque as the first course of an elegant dinner party. Follow with Roasted Halibut with Pistachio-Parmesan Crust (page 152) and Pasta with Leeks and Peas (page 171).

INGREDIENTS:

2 OUNCES DRIED WILD MUSHROOMS, SHIITAKE OR PORCINI

6 CUPS CHICKEN OR VEGETABLE BROTH

3 TABLESPOONS UNSALTED BUTTER

¼ POUND THICK-CUT PANCETTA OR BACON, CUT INTO ½-INCH DICE

1 LEEK, WHITE AND LIGHT GREEN PARTS ONLY, CLEANED AND FINELY CHOPPED

1 POUND FRESH CREMINI MUSH-ROOMS, THINLY SLICED

ONE 8-OUNCE YUKON GOLD POTATO, PEELED AND CUT INTO 2-INCH DICE

1 GARLIC CLOVE, MINCED

SALT AND FRESHLY GROUND WHITE PEPPER

1 TABLESPOON PLUS 1 TEASPOON SOY SAUCE

½ CUP HALF-AND-HALF

⅓ CUP DRY SHERRY, OR TO TASTE

2 TABLESPOONS FINELY CHOPPED FRESH PARSLEY FOR GARNISH

1. In a medium saucepan, combine the dried mushrooms and broth. Bring to a boil over high heat, cover, reduce the heat to medium, and simmer for 5 minutes. Or combine in a large glass measuring cup, loosely cover with plastic wrap, and microwave for 4 minutes. Set aside to infuse.

2. In a medium soup pot, melt 1 tablespoon of the butter over medium heat. Add the pancetta and fry, turning with a spatula, for about 4 minutes, or until crisp on all sides. Transfer to paper towels to drain. Discard the fat in the pot. Return to medium-high heat and melt the remaining 2 tablespoons butter. Sauté the leek for 3 to 4 minutes, or until soft. Add the fresh mushrooms, diced potato, and garlic and sauté for 3 minutes, or until the potato is softened.

3. Remove the dried mushrooms from the broth, reserving the broth, and add them to the pot.

Pour the broth through a fine-mesh strainer into the pot. Season with salt and pepper and add the soy sauce. Simmer, partially covered, for 15 minutes.

4. With a hand blender, process the soup until it is roughly puréed with some texture remaining. Add the half-and-half and sherry and simmer for 2 minutes. Taste and adjust the seasonings.

5. To serve, ladle the bisque into soup bowls and garnish with the pancetta croutons and parsley. Serve immediately.

ADVANCE PREPARATION:
Make the bisque up to 3 days ahead, cover, and refrigerate. Reheat gently, adjusting the seasonings. Make the croutons up to 6 hours ahead, cover, and refrigerate. Reheat in the microwave for 30 seconds, or until hot and crisp. The bisque does not freeze well because it contains half-and-half, which will curdle when defrosted and reheated.

PERSIMMON AND WINTER SQUASH SOUP WITH LEMON-NUTMEG CREAM

SERVES 4 TO 6

My friend Connie Bryson is an amazing artist and also a creative cook. She shared with me her inspired holiday soup combining crispy, sweet Fuyu persimmons with velvety orange winter squash. I fell in love with the complementary flavors and the spectacular color. In the cream, I prefer to use Meyer lemons, which are a little sweeter and less acidic than the variety commonly found in supermarkets. Serve this soup in shallow bowls as a first course at dinner or as a simple lunch with Baby Greens with Autumn Fruit and Warm Goat Cheese (page 77). I also like to offer small mugs or espresso cups of the soup when company arrives.

INGREDIENTS:

2 TABLESPOONS OLIVE OIL

2 LEEKS, WHITE AND LIGHT GREEN PARTS ONLY, CLEANED AND FINELY CHOPPED

ONE 1-POUND BAG PEELED, SEEDED, AND DICED BUTTERNUT SQUASH, OR ONE 2-POUND BUTTERNUT SQUASH, PEELED, SEEDED, AND DICED

4 FUYU PERSIMMONS, PEELED AND CUT INTO 2-INCH CUBES

2 GARLIC CLOVES, MINCED

5 CUPS CHICKEN OR VEGETABLE BROTH

1 TABLESPOON FRESH THYME LEAVES, CHOPPED

SALT AND FRESHLY GROUND BLACK PEPPER

————

LEMON-NUTMEG CREAM

¼ CUP SOUR CREAM OR CRÈME FRAÎCHE

GRATED ZEST OF 1 LEMON

1 TEASPOON FRESH LEMON JUICE

FRESHLY GRATED NUTMEG

————

2 TABLESPOONS FINELY CHOPPED FRESH CHIVES FOR GARNISH

1. In a large saucepan, warm the oil over medium-high heat. Sauté the leeks for 5 minutes, or until softened. Add the squash and persimmons and sauté for 3 minutes, or until nicely coated with the oil. Add the garlic and sauté for 1 minute. Stir in the broth, thyme, and salt and pepper to taste. Bring to a boil, reduce the heat to medium-low, cover, and simmer for 20 to 25 minutes, or until the squash and persimmons are tender.

2. Meanwhile, make the lemon-nutmeg cream: In a small bowl, stir together the cream and lemon zest and juice. Season to taste with the nutmeg and stir to blend.

3. Purée the soup in the pan with a hand blender, or purée in a blender or a food processor fitted with the metal blade and return the soup to the pan. Taste and adjust the seasonings.

4. To serve, ladle the soup into bowls. Swirl about 1 tablespoon of the lemon-nutmeg cream into each serving and garnish with the chives.

ADVANCE PREPARATION:
Make the soup up to 3 days ahead, cover, and refrigerate. Reheat gently. This soup also freezes well. Defrost, reheat, and adjust the seasonings. The lemon-nutmeg cream should be made just before serving.

THE CLEVER COOK COULD:
- Use a total of 1½ pounds peeled, seeded, and diced winter squash if persimmons are not available.
- Add a pinch of ancho or chipotle chile powder and lime juice, instead of lemon juice, to the cream, and omit the nutmeg, for a spicy flavor.

FENNEL, POTATO, AND CARROT SOUP

⋖ SERVES 8 ⋗

The faint anise taste of fennel is a subtle backdrop for the
potato and carrot purée. Serve the soup as an elegant beginning to
a dinner party or in small cups as your guests arrive. It also makes
an interesting way to start a luncheon. Follow
with Winter Chopped Salad (page 80).

INGREDIENTS:

2 TABLESPOONS OLIVE OIL

2 ONIONS, FINELY CHOPPED

3 FENNEL BULBS, STEMMED, THINLY
SLICED, AND COARSELY CHOPPED

2 GARLIC CLOVES, MINCED

1 TEASPOON SERIOUSLY SIMPLE
SEASONING SALT (PAGE 208)

FRESHLY GROUND BLACK PEPPER

4 CARROTS, PEELED AND CUT INTO
2-INCH PIECES

4 WHITE POTATOES, PEELED
AND CUT INTO 2-INCH PIECES

8 CUPS CHICKEN OR VEGETABLE
BROTH

4 TABLESPOONS FRESH LEMON JUICE

4 TABLESPOONS FINELY CHOPPED
FRESH PARSLEY

GARLIC CROUTONS FOR GARNISH

1. In a large saucepan or Dutch
oven, heat the oil over medium-
high heat. Sauté the onions for
5 minutes, or until softened. Add
the fennel and sauté for 5 minutes,
or until slightly softened. Add the
garlic and salt, season with pepper,
and sauté for 1 minute. Add the
carrots, the potatoes, and 7 cups
of the broth, and stir to combine.
Partially cover and simmer over
medium heat for 30 to 35 minutes,
or until the potatoes are tender.

2. Purée the soup in the pan
with a hand blender, or purée in a
blender or a food processor fitted
with the metal blade and return to
the pan. Add the remaining 1 cup
broth and bring to a simmer over
medium heat. Add the lemon juice
and 2 tablespoons of the parsley, and
cook for 3 minutes. Taste and
adjust the seasonings.

3. To serve, ladle the soup into
bowls, and garnish with croutons
and the remaining parsley.

ADVANCE PREPARATION:
Make up to 3 days ahead, cover,
and refrigerate. Reheat gently. This
soup also freezes well; defrost,
reheat, and adjust the seasonings.

THE CLEVER COOK COULD:
- Stir in 2 tablespoons tomato
  paste when adding the broth
  in step 1.
- Add 1 cup drained canned
  garbanzo beans just before
  puréeing the soup.
- Omit the fennel and add
  2 peeled and coarsely chopped
  parsnips or 4 sliced zucchini.
- Garnish the soup with finely
  chopped fennel fronds, freshly
  grated Parmesan cheese, or
  sour cream.

NEW YEAR'S EVE ONION SOUP WITH PARMESAN-GRUYÈRE CROUTONS

SERVES 6

What a way to say good-bye to the old year and herald in the new. I love to serve this soup just before or after midnight, along with chilled Champagne or sparkling wine. It can give you energy to carry on celebrating, or make a satisfying end to the evening. This version of onion soup is easier to make than classic French recipes because it uses a garnish of cheese croutons rather than melting the cheese in the broiler. You'll save a step since you don't have to put the soup under the broiler. You can vary the croutons by substituting fresh goat cheese, Teleme, or Italian fontina for the cheeses called for here.

INGREDIENTS:

2 TABLESPOONS OLIVE OIL

4 LARGE RED ONIONS, THINLY SLICED

1 TEASPOON SUGAR

4 LEEKS, WHITE AND LIGHT GREEN PARTS ONLY, CLEANED AND THINLY SLICED

4 GARLIC CLOVES, MINCED

10 CUPS CHICKEN OR BEEF BROTH

½ CUP DRY WHITE WINE

1 BAY LEAF

½ TEASPOON MINCED FRESH THYME, OR ¼ TEASPOON DRIED THYME

SALT AND FRESHLY GROUND BLACK PEPPER

————

PARMESAN-GRUYÈRE CROUTONS

TWELVE ½-INCH-THICK SLICES BAGUETTE

½ CUP SHREDDED GRUYÈRE CHEESE

¼ CUP FRESHLY GRATED PARMESAN CHEESE

————

2 TABLESPOONS FINELY CHOPPED FRESH PARSLEY FOR GARNISH

1. In a large nonaluminum saucepan, heat the oil over medium-low heat. Sauté the onions, stirring occasionally, for about 15 minutes, or until wilted. Add the sugar and leeks and cook, stirring frequently, for 30 to 45 minutes, or until dark golden and caramelized. You may need to raise the heat to medium to reach the desired color.

2. Add the garlic and sauté for 1 minute. Add the broth, white wine, bay leaf, and thyme. Partially cover and simmer for 30 minutes, or until the flavors are nicely blended. Season with salt and pepper. Taste and adjust the seasonings. Discard the bay leaf.

3. Meanwhile, make the croutons: Preheat the broiler. Place the bread slices in a single layer on a baking sheet and toast for 1½ to 2 minutes, or until golden. Sprinkle each slice with equal amounts of Gruyère and Parmesan. Just before serving, broil the croutons for 1 to 2 minutes, or until the cheeses are just melted.

4. Ladle the soup into deep soup bowls and float 2 croutons on each serving. Sprinkle with the parsley. Serve immediately.

ADVANCE PREPARATION:

Make the soup 3 days ahead, cover, and refrigerate. Reheat gently. The soup also freezes well. Defrost, reheat, and adjust the seasonings. Make the croutons through step 3 up to 4 hours ahead, cover, and keep at room temperature.

CHICKEN-VEGETABLE SOUP WITH HERBED MATZO BALLS

SERVES 6 TO 8

During the Jewish holidays, the menu often begins with this beloved soup. Every person who makes it has his or her own special touch, whether it's the herbs or vegetables or how to make the matzo balls. This recipe gives you a head start because you begin with a good-quality store-bought broth.

INGREDIENTS:

FOUR ¾-POUND BONE-IN, SKINLESS CHICKEN BREAST HALVES

8 CUPS CHICKEN BROTH

6 CUPS WATER

3 LEEKS, WHITE AND LIGHT GREEN PARTS ONLY, CLEANED AND FINELY CHOPPED

4 CARROTS, PEELED AND CUT INTO ½-INCH-THICK SLICES

2 CELERY STALKS, CUT INTO ½-INCH-THICK SLICES

2 PARSNIPS, PEELED AND CUT INTO ½-INCH-THICK SLICES

2 TABLESPOONS COARSELY CHOPPED FRESH MINT

4 CHERRY TOMATOES, HALVED

SALT AND FRESHLY GROUND BLACK PEPPER

MATZO BALLS

¼ CUP RENDERED CHICKEN FAT OR CANOLA OIL

4 LARGE EGGS, SLIGHTLY BEATEN

1 CUP MATZO MEAL

2 TABLESPOONS FINELY CHOPPED FRESH PARSLEY

2 TABLESPOONS FINELY CHOPPED FRESH CHIVES

1¾ TEASPOONS SALT

¼ CUP SELTZER WATER OR SPARKLING WATER

2 TABLESPOONS FINELY CHOPPED FRESH PARSLEY FOR GARNISH

1. In a large soup pot, combine the chicken, broth, and water. Bring to a boil over medium-high heat, skimming any foam from the surface. Add the leeks, carrots, celery, parsnips, mint, and tomatoes. Partially cover, reduce the heat to low, and simmer for about 30 minutes, or until the chicken is cooked through and the vegetables are just tender. Periodically skim the foam from the surface. Season with salt and pepper.

2. Remove the chicken from the soup and let cool slightly. With your hands, remove the meat from the bones, discarding the bones and cartilage. Tear the chicken into bite-size pieces and return to the pot. Cover and refrigerate.

3. Make the matzo balls: In a medium bowl, whisk together the fat and eggs. Add the matzo meal, herbs, and salt and stir well. Add the seltzer water and mix well.

continued on next page

. . . continued

Cover and refrigerate for 30 minutes, or until the dough thickens.

4. Fill a large, wide pot three-
fourths full of water. Bring to a boil
over medium-high heat. To shape
the matzo balls, using your hands,
roll the dough very lightly into
1½-inch balls. (The more you roll
them, the tougher and heavier they
will become.) Reduce the heat to
medium and drop the balls into the
barely simmering water. Cover and
cook for 25 to 30 minutes, or until
cooked through. Remove the matzo
balls to a bowl and set aside.

5. To serve, remove the soup
from the refrigerator and carefully
lift the fat layer from the surface.
Reheat the soup over medium
heat for 15 to 20 minutes. Taste
and adjust the seasonings. Add
the matzo balls and cook for
3 to 5 minutes, or just until heated
through. Serve the soup in large
bowls and garnish with the parsley.

ADVANCE PREPARATION:
Make the soup up to 3 days
ahead, cover, and refrigerate.
Make the matzo balls up to
4 hours ahead, cover, and keep
at room temperature.

THE CLEVER COOK COULD:
○ For a lighter version, strain
the soup and serve only with
the matzo balls. Reserve the
chicken and use for making
a chicken salad.

GREEN LENTIL SOUP WITH SAUSAGES AND RED PEPPERS

≈ SERVES 6 ≈

You will want to make this satisfying soup again and again. It is a terrific main-course soup for a Sunday supper or a chilly afternoon's lunch. Accompany it with a salad such as Two-Endive Salad with Pear, Walnuts, and Blue Cheese (page 79) or Winter Chopped Salad (page 80).

INGREDIENTS:

2 TABLESPOONS OLIVE OIL

1 LARGE ONION, FINELY CHOPPED

3 CARROTS, PEELED AND FINELY CHOPPED

2 CELERY STALKS, FINELY CHOPPED

1 SMALL RED BELL PEPPER, SEEDED AND FINELY DICED

2 GARLIC CLOVES, MINCED

1½ CUPS GREEN LENTILS, RINSED AND PICKED OVER

8 CUPS VEGETABLE OR CHICKEN BROTH, OR MORE IF NEEDED

4 TABLESPOONS FINELY CHOPPED FRESH PARSLEY

SALT AND FRESHLY GROUND BLACK PEPPER

2 TABLESPOONS DRY SHERRY

½ POUND VERY THINLY SLICED COOKED CHICKEN SAUSAGES OR SPICY TURKEY SAUSAGES

1. In a large soup pot, heat the oil over medium heat. Sauté the onion for about 3 minutes, or until softened. Add the carrots, celery, and bell pepper and sauté for 3 to 4 minutes, or until slightly softened. Add the garlic and sauté for 1 minute.

2. Add the lentils, 8 cups broth, and 2 tablespoons of the parsley and bring to a simmer. Season with salt and pepper. Reduce the heat to medium-low, cover, and cook, stirring occasionally, for about 40 minutes, or until the lentils are tender. Test by pushing the lentils with the back of a wooden spoon; if they break up easily, they are cooked. You may need to add more broth.

3. With a hand blender, coarsely process the soup, retaining some texture. If the soup seems too thick, add 1 cup of broth or water. Add the sherry and sausages, raise the heat to medium-high, and cook for 3 to 5 minutes, or until the alcohol has evaporated and the sausages are cooked through. Taste and adjust the seasonings. Ladle into soup bowls, garnish with the remaining 2 tablespoons parsley, and serve immediately.

ADVANCE PREPARATION:
Make up to 3 days in advance, cover, and refrigerate. Reheat gently. The soup also freezes well; defrost, reheat, and adjust the seasonings.

THE CLEVER COOK COULD:
- Increase the sausages to 1½ pounds and serve the soup as a main course.
- Add fresh winter herbs like savory or thyme.
- Omit the sausages and purée the soup, strain, and serve as a simple first course.

GOULASH SOUP

⋅⋚ SERVES 6 ⋛⋅

After graduating from college, I traveled throughout Europe and ended up in Vienna for a few weeks. It was November and very cold. I ordered goulash soup in a small family restaurant and then returned to order it every day thereafter, trying to discern the ingredients. Caraway seeds, red pepper, and paprika were the key. A finishing swirl of sour cream made the fragrant, hearty soup irresistible. It is perfect for a chilly night along with some really good country bread and a simple green salad.

INGREDIENTS:

3 TABLESPOONS OLIVE OIL

4 LEEKS, WHITE AND LIGHT GREEN PARTS ONLY, CLEANED AND FINELY CHOPPED

2 TEASPOONS CARAWAY SEEDS

1 RED BELL PEPPER, SEEDED AND CHOPPED

1 POUND BEEF STEW MEAT, CUT INTO ½-INCH PIECES

3 TABLESPOONS HUNGARIAN SWEET PAPRIKA

8 CUPS CHICKEN, BEEF, OR VEGETABLE BROTH

ONE 14½-OUNCE CAN DICED TOMATOES WITH JUICE

3 GARLIC CLOVES, MINCED

ONE ¾- TO 1-POUND YUKON GOLD POTATO, PEELED AND DICED

2 CARROTS, PEELED AND SLICED

1 PARSNIP, PEELED AND SLICED

SALT AND FRESHLY GROUND BLACK PEPPER

¼ CUP FINELY CHOPPED FRESH PARSLEY

½ CUP SOUR CREAM FOR GARNISH

1. In a large, heavy pot, heat the oil over medium-high heat. Sauté the leeks and caraway seeds for 5 minutes, or until softened. Add the bell pepper and sauté for 2 minutes, or until softened.

2. Add the beef and paprika and sauté for 7 to 10 minutes, or until the beef is evenly browned on all sides. Add the broth, raise the heat to high, and deglaze the pot by scraping up the brown bits. Reduce the heat to low, partially cover, and simmer for 30 to 40 minutes, or until the meat is tender.

3. Stir in the tomatoes, garlic, potato, carrots, and parsnip. Season with salt and pepper, partially cover, and simmer for 20 minutes, or until all the vegetables are tender.

4. With a hand blender, coarsely process the soup, retaining some texture. Stir in the parsley. Taste and adjust the seasonings.

5. To serve, ladle the soup into soup bowls, garnish each with a dollop of sour cream, and serve immediately.

ADVANCE PREPARATION:
Make up to 3 days ahead, cover, and refrigerate. Reheat gently and adjust the seasonings. The soup also freezes well; defrost, reheat gently, and adjust the seasonings.

BABY GREENS WITH AUTUMN FRUIT AND WARM GOAT CHEESE

SERVES 8

This is a special salad full of autumn's finest. I like to serve it as a starter for an elegant dinner that includes Standing Rib Roast with Horseradish Cream and Cabernet Sauce (page 134) and Perfect Mashed Potatoes (page 185). For dessert, offer Chocolate-Toffee Pie (page 201).

INGREDIENTS:

ONE 8-OUNCE LOG FRESH GOAT CHEESE, CUT INTO 8 EQUAL DISKS

OLIVE OIL SPRAY

1 CUP PANKO OR OTHER DRIED COARSE BREAD CRUMBS

———

VINAIGRETTE

1 SHALLOT, FINELY CHOPPED

1 GARLIC CLOVE, MINCED

1 TEASPOON WHOLE-GRAIN MUSTARD

¼ CUP POMEGRANATE OR RED WINE VINEGAR

1 TABLESPOON FINELY CHOPPED FRESH PARSLEY

1 TABLESPOON FINELY CHOPPED FRESH CHIVES

¾ CUP OLIVE OIL

1 TABLESPOON HEAVY CREAM OR PLAIN YOGURT

SALT AND FRESHLY GROUND BLACK PEPPER

———

¾ POUND MIXED BABY GREENS

8 MEDJOOL DATES, PITTED AND CHOPPED

1 PINK LADY APPLE, PEELED, CORED, AND DICED

⅓ CUP POMEGRANATE SEEDS

1. Place the goat cheese disks on a broiler pan and lightly coat with olive oil spray. Pour the panko on a plate and roll the disks in the panko, lightly pressing the crumbs onto the cheese. Return to the pan. Refrigerate for 30 minutes.

2. Meanwhile, make the vinaigrette: In a medium bowl, combine the shallot, garlic, mustard, vinegar, parsley, and chives. Whisk until well blended. (Or place in a food processor fitted with the metal blade and process until well blended). Slowly pour in the oil, whisking (or processing) until blended. Whisk in the cream. Season with salt and pepper. Taste and adjust the seasonings.

3. Preheat the oven to 400°F. In a large salad bowl, combine the greens, dates, apple, and pomegranate seeds.

4. Bake the cheese for 5 to 7 minutes, or until the crumbs are nicely browned and the cheese is warmed through.

5. To serve, pour enough vinaigrette over the salad to moisten and toss to combine. Arrange on salad plates and top each salad with a goat cheese disk. Drizzle with more vinaigrette, if desired, and serve.

ADVANCE PREPARATION:
Make the vinaigrette up to 1 week ahead, cover, and refrigerate. Bring to room temperature and whisk before using. Make the salad up to 2 hours ahead, cover, and refrigerate.

THE CLEVER COOK COULD:
○ Use any remaining vinaigrette on different greens like spinach and arugula, or as a marinade for chicken.

TWO-ENDIVE SALAD WITH PEAR, WALNUTS, AND BLUE CHEESE

Frisée and Belgian endive are a good combination of textures and flavors because both are from the chicory family. In this appetizer salad, pear and toasted walnuts add a fresh, crunchy dimension to the pungent greens. If you want a more delicate blue cheese flavor, freeze the cheese for 15 minutes and then grate it over the salad just before serving.

INGREDIENTS:

VINAIGRETTE

3 TABLESPOONS SHERRY VINEGAR

1 TABLESPOON FRESH LEMON JUICE

2 TEASPOONS HONEY DIJON MUSTARD

½ CUP OLIVE OIL

SALT AND FRESHLY GROUND BLACK PEPPER

———

½ CUP WALNUTS OR CANDIED WALNUTS OR PECANS

1 HEAD FRISÉE OR BABY CURLY ENDIVE, TORN INTO BITE-SIZE PIECES

6 HEADS BELGIAN ENDIVE, ENDS REMOVED AND CUT LENGTHWISE INTO THIN STRIPS

1 PEAR SUCH AS ANJOU, BOSC, OR COMICE, PEELED, CORED, AND SLICED

½ CUP CRUMBLED BLUE CHEESE

1. Make the vinaigrette: In a small bowl, whisk together the vinegar, lemon juice, and mustard. Slowly whisk in the oil until emulsified. Season with salt and pepper. Taste and adjust the seasonings.

2. If using plain walnuts, preheat the oven to 350°F. Place the walnuts on a baking sheet and toast for 7 to 10 minutes, or until lightly browned and aromatic.

3. In a salad bowl, combine the frisée and endive with the pear and walnuts. Sprinkle the blue cheese over the salad.

4. Drizzle with the vinaigrette, toss well, and serve.

ADVANCE PREPARATION:

Make up to 4 hours ahead through step 3, cover, and refrigerate. Keep the vinaigrette at room temperature.

WINTER CHOPPED SALAD

SERVES 8 AS A FIRST COURSE, 6 AS A MAIN COURSE

With a little help from a dish always served at the Restaurant at the Getty Center in Los Angeles, I've reinterpreted a chopped salad using winter ingredients. To speed preparation, you can purchase a rotisserie chicken rather than cook the chicken breasts yourself. I serve this salad for a casual weekend brunch, along with Mushroom and Potato Bisque with Pancetta Croutons (page 66). It is also good on a buffet lunch table.

INGREDIENTS:

DRESSING

1 TABLESPOON DIJON MUSTARD

3 TABLESPOONS APPLE CIDER VINEGAR

1 TABLESPOON HONEY

½ CUP OLIVE OIL

SALT AND FRESHLY GROUND BLACK PEPPER

———————

1 HEAD RADICCHIO, CORED AND FINELY CHOPPED

2 HEADS ROMAINE LETTUCE, LIGHT GREEN AND WHITE LEAVES ONLY, FINELY CHOPPED

1¼ POUNDS COOKED CHICKEN BREASTS, SKIN AND BONES REMOVED AND CUT INTO 1-INCH DICE (ABOUT 3 CUPS)

1 FUJI, GALA, OR PINK LADY APPLE, PEELED, CORED, AND CUT INTO ¼-INCH DICE

1 CUP DRIED CRANBERRIES

1 CUP CANDIED PECANS OR WALNUTS, COARSELY CHOPPED

1 CUP CRUMBLED BLUE OR FRESH GOAT CHEESE

FRESHLY GROUND BLACK PEPPER (OPTIONAL)

1. Make the dressing: In a small bowl, whisk together the mustard, vinegar, honey, olive oil, and salt and pepper to taste. Taste and adjust the seasonings.

2. Place the radicchio, romaine, chicken, apple, cranberries, nuts, and cheese in a large salad bowl.

3. Pour the dressing over the salad and toss to coat. Sprinkle with pepper (if desired) and serve.

ADVANCE PREPARATION:
Make the dressing up to 2 days ahead, cover, and keep at room temperature. Whisk well before using. Make the salad up to 4 hours ahead, cover, and refrigerate.

THE CLEVER COOK COULD:
- Substitute 3 cups diced cooked turkey for the chicken.
- Add 6 strips of bacon, fried until crisp and crumbled.
- Omit the chicken and serve the salad as a first course.
- If you're not a fan of chopped salad, tear the lettuce and radicchio leaves into bite-size pieces instead of finely chopping them.

MIXED GREENS WITH PERSIMMONS, PROSCIUTTO, AND SHAVED PARMESAN

❧ SERVES 6 TO 8 ❧

I love this salad for holiday entertaining because it is an appetizer and a first course rolled into one. You can serve the salad as part of a buffet or plate it for a dinner party. For the greens, I like to use a mix that includes arugula and radicchio along with young, tender lettuce leaves. A swivel peeler is the best tool for shaving the Parmesan cheese.

INGREDIENTS:

½ POUND MIXED GREENS

4 HEADS BELGIAN ENDIVE, ENDS REMOVED AND THINLY SLICED CROSSWISE

3 FUYU PERSIMMONS, PEELED, CORED, AND CUT INTO 1-INCH-THICK SLICES

3 OUNCES THINLY SLICED PROSCIUTTO OR SERRANO HAM, SHREDDED

¼ POUND PARMESAN CHEESE, CUT INTO SHAVINGS

———————

DRESSING

3 TABLESPOONS BALSAMIC VINEGAR

1 TABLESPOON WHITE BALSAMIC VINEGAR

2 TEASPOONS DIJON MUSTARD

½ CUP OLIVE OIL

SALT AND FRESHLY GROUND BLACK PEPPER

1. Place the greens and endive in a large salad bowl. Scatter the persimmons, prosciutto, and Parmesan on top.

2. Make the dressing: In a small bowl, whisk together the vinegars, mustard, olive oil, and salt and pepper to taste until emulsified. Taste and adjust the seasonings.

3. Pour enough dressing over the salad to moisten and toss to coat. Serve immediately.

ADVANCE PREPARATION:
Make up to 4 hours ahead through step 2. Cover the salad and refrigerate. Remove from the refrigerator 30 minutes before serving. Keep the dressing at room temperature.

LIME-MINT SLAW

SERVES 6

This pretty version of coleslaw is perfect for the holidays. The light green cabbage contrasts with the orange carrots and the garnish of green herbs and bright red pomegranate seeds. Serve the slaw with Slow-Roasted Salmon with Miso Vinaigrette (page 151) or on a buffet with other salads.

INGREDIENTS:

DRESSING

2 GARLIC CLOVES, MINCED

SALT AND FRESHLY GROUND BLACK PEPPER

½ TEASPOON SUGAR

⅓ CUP FRESH LIME JUICE

⅓ CUP OLIVE OIL

___

ONE 1-POUND PACKAGE SHREDDED CABBAGE AND CARROT COLESLAW (ABOUT 6 CUPS)

1 TABLESPOON FINELY CHOPPED FRESH DILL

2 TABLESPOONS FINELY CHOPPED FRESH MINT

2 TABLESPOONS FINELY CHOPPED FRESH CILANTRO

2 TABLESPOONS POMEGRANATE SEEDS FOR GARNISH

2 TABLESPOONS CURRANTS FOR GARNISH

1. Make the dressing: In a small bowl, combine the garlic, salt and pepper to taste, sugar, and lime juice. Slowly whisk in the oil until blended. Taste and adjust the seasonings.

2. Place the coleslaw in a large serving bowl and sprinkle with the herbs.

3. Pour the dressing over the salad and toss to coat. Garnish with the pomegranate seeds and currants. Serve immediately.

ADVANCE PREPARATION:
Make up to 2 hours ahead through step 2. Cover and refrigerate the salad. Keep the dressing at room temperature.

___

THE CLEVER COOK COULD:
- Serve the slaw as a bed for simple grilled fish or chicken breasts.
- Add shredded cooked chicken or turkey and use as a main course salad or filling for pita bread or flour tortillas.

___

BREAKFAST AND BRUNCH

MAPLE OATMEAL WITH DRIED FRUIT AND GRANOLA

❄ SERVES 4 ❄

Using quick-cooking steel-cut oats takes much of the time out of making this comforting cereal. Dried fruit and granola offer a wonderful textural contrast to the creamy oatmeal. Be sure to use a large saucepan as the milk can easily boil over. Measure everything but the milk the night before, and this will take just minutes from the stove to the table.

INGREDIENTS:

4 CUPS MILK, PLUS WARM MILK FOR SERVING

2 TEASPOONS VANILLA EXTRACT

1 TEASPOON GROUND CINNAMON

⅓ CUP PURE MAPLE SYRUP, PLUS MORE FOR SERVING

1⅓ CUPS QUICK-COOKING STEEL-CUT IRISH OATMEAL

½ CUP CHOPPED MIXED DRIED FRUIT SUCH AS APRICOTS, CRANBERRIES, CHERRIES, AND PLUMS

½ CUP GRANOLA

1. In a large saucepan, combine the 4 cups milk, vanilla, cinnamon, and ⅓ cup syrup. Whisk to blend. Bring to a simmer over medium heat.

2. Add the oatmeal and cook, stirring constantly, for 5 to 7 minutes, or until the desired thickness and texture. Add the dried fruit and granola and stir to combine. Cook for 1 minute. Spoon into shallow bowls and serve immediately with maple syrup and warm milk on the side.

SPICED PUMPKIN WAFFLES

❄ SERVES 4 TO 6 ❄

Waffles are a good solution for serving guests who might want breakfast at different times. Just keep the waffle iron on and let them make their own waffles. These waffles, light and airy with a crispy exterior, will fill the kitchen with the aromas associated with holidays. Grilled or baked chicken-apple sausages make a great accompaniment.

INGREDIENTS:

2½ CUPS ALL-PURPOSE FLOUR

1 TABLESPOON BAKING POWDER

½ TEASPOON BAKING SODA

½ TEASPOON SALT

1 TABLESPOON PUMPKIN PIE SPICE

PINCH FRESHLY GRATED NUTMEG

4 LARGE EGGS

½ CUP PACKED DARK BROWN SUGAR

1 CUP PUMPKIN PURÉE

¼ CUP (½ STICK) UNSALTED BUTTER, MELTED

2 CUPS BUTTERMILK

1 TEASPOON VANILLA EXTRACT

CANOLA OIL FOR COATING

POWDERED SUGAR FOR SERVING

PURE MAPLE SYRUP, WARMED, FOR SERVING

WARM SPICED PERSIMMON COMPOTE (PAGE 215; OPTIONAL)

1. In a large bowl, lightly whisk together the flour, baking powder, baking soda, salt, pumpkin pie spice, and nutmeg.

2. In another large bowl, whisk together the eggs and brown sugar until any lumps are dissolved and well blended. Add the pumpkin purée, butter, buttermilk, and vanilla and whisk until smooth. Add the flour mixture and blend until smooth.

3. Preheat the oven to 200°F. Heat a waffle iron according to the manufacturer's directions. Lightly grease it with a paper towel or pastry brush dipped in a little oil. Pour in enough batter just to fill the iron and spread it evenly, then close the waffle iron. Cook until the waffle iron opens easily and the waffles are golden brown on the outside and cooked through inside. Remove to a platter and keep warm in the oven while you cook the remaining waffles.

4. Serve the waffles sprinkled with powdered sugar and drizzled with maple syrup. Garnish with a dollop of persimmon compote, if desired.

ADVANCE PREPARATION:
Make up to 1 day ahead through step 2, cover, and refrigerate. Remove the batter from the refrigerator 30 minutes before cooking. Whisk the batter and add a few tablespoons of milk if it is too thick. The waffles can be frozen for 1 month. Reheat in a 350°F oven until warmed through, about 15 minutes.

THE CLEVER COOK COULD:
- Serve the waffles with Maple-Pear Applesauce (page 214).
- Make pancakes by adding a few tablespoons of milk to thin the batter and cooking the pancakes in an oiled nonstick skillet.
- Serve the waffles as a dessert with a scoop of pumpkin ice cream and warm Caramel Sauce (page 218).

PANETTONE BREAKFAST PUDDING WITH EGGNOG CUSTARD

❅ SERVES 8 ❅

In this festive pudding, Italian fruit bread called panettone takes the place of plain bread, and eggnog fills in for milk. This is a wonderful Christmas morning treat since all the preparation is done the night before, leaving only the baking. I like to serve the pudding with grilled sausages or crispy bacon. A pitcher of mixed orange and grapefruit juices with a splash of pomegranate juice would round out the celebration. The recipe needs to be started two days ahead so the panettone cubes can dry out and the pudding can set before baking.

INGREDIENTS:

ONE 1½-POUND BOX PANETTONE, CUT INTO 1½-INCH CUBES (ABOUT 8 CUPS)

6 LARGE EGGS

⅓ CUP BAKING SUGAR

4 CUPS EGGNOG

1 TABLESPOON VANILLA EXTRACT

1 TEASPOON PUMPKIN PIE SPICE

PINCH FRESHLY GRATED NUTMEG

POWDERED SUGAR FOR GARNISH

WARM SPICED PERSIMMON COMPOTE (PAGE 215; OPTIONAL)

1. One day before preparing the pudding, place the panettone cubes on a baking sheet and let stand at room temperature overnight, or until the cubes are dried out.

2. The next day, butter a 9-by-13-inch baking dish. Arrange the cubes in the dish.

3. In a large bowl, beat the eggs with an electric mixer on medium speed or a whisk until frothy. Add the baking sugar and beat for 3 minutes, or until thick and light lemon colored. Add the eggnog, reduce the speed to low, and beat to combine. Add the vanilla, pumpkin pie spice, and nutmeg and mix to combine.

4. Ladle the eggnog mixture over the panettone cubes, using your fingers, if necessary, to distribute the ingredients evenly. Cover with aluminum foil and refrigerate overnight.

5. The next morning, remove the baking dish from the refrigerator 1 hour before baking and preheat the oven to 375°F. Use a wooden spoon to push the cubes down and evenly distribute the eggnog mix-

ture. Bake for 20 to 25 minutes.
Open the oven door and, wearing
heavy oven mitts, push the panettone down with the wooden spoon.
The remaining liquid will rise.
Spoon it evenly over the cubes.
Bake for 15 to 20 more minutes,
or until a skewer inserted into the
center comes out barely clean. Let
rest for 10 minutes. Sprinkle with
the powdered sugar. Serve in bowls
with the Warm Spiced Persimmon
Compote, if desired.

ADVANCE PREPARATION:
Make up to 4 hours ahead, cover,
and keep at room temperature.
Reheat in a 350°F oven for
15 minutes, if desired.

THE CLEVER COOK COULD:
○ Serve the pudding for dessert,
  garnished with whipped cream
  flavored with rum.

SAVORY BREAD PUDDING WITH BACON, PEPPERS, AND SPINACH

❄ SERVES 6 TO 8 ❄

In this quintessential Christmas brunch dish, crisp, mahogany-red bacon and red peppers contrast with bright green spinach leaves. The pudding makes breakfast or brunch a one-dish meal, though I like to serve it with a winter fruit platter. Remember to start the recipe two days in advance, as the bread cubes need to dry out and the pudding must set before baking.

INGREDIENTS:

ONE 14-OUNCE LOAF OLIVE CIABATTA, CRUSTS REMOVED, CUT INTO 1½-INCH CUBES

½ POUND APPLE WOOD-SMOKED BACON, CUT INTO 2-INCH PIECES

¾ CUP JARRED ROASTED RED PEPPERS, RINSED, DRAINED, AND CHOPPED

2 CUPS SPINACH LEAVES

2 CUPS SHREDDED CHEDDAR CHEESE, PLUS ¼ CUP FOR TOPPING

6 EGGS

4 CUPS MILK OR HALF-AND-HALF

2 TEASPOONS DIJON MUSTARD

SALT AND FRESHLY GROUND BLACK PEPPER

1. One day before preparing the pudding, place the bread cubes on a baking sheet and let stand at room temperature overnight, or until the cubes are dried out.

2. The next day, in a large skillet, cook the bacon over medium-high heat, turning once, for 5 minutes, or until evenly brown and crisp. Remove to paper towels to drain.

3. Butter a 9-by-13-inch baking dish. Arrange the cubes in the dish. Scatter the bacon, peppers, and spinach leaves evenly over the cubes. Sprinkle with the 2 cups cheese. With a large spoon, evenly distribute the ingredients.

4. In a large bowl, whisk together or beat with an electric mixer on medium speed the eggs, milk, mustard, and salt and pepper to taste until well blended. Ladle the milk mixture over the bread, using your fingers, if necessary, to press the bread into the liquid. Sprinkle with the ¼ cup cheese. Cover with aluminum foil and refrigerate overnight.

5. The next morning, remove the baking dish from the refrigerator 1 hour before baking and preheat the oven to 350°F. Bake for 45 to 50 minutes, or until slightly puffed, set, and browned on the top. If the center is still underdone, push the bread down with a wooden spoon to help the bread absorb the liquid. Bake for a few more minutes. Let rest for a few minutes and then cut into squares. Serve slightly warm or at room temperature.

ADVANCE PREPARATION:
Make up to 4 hours ahead, cover, and keep at room temperature. Reheat in a 350°F oven for 15 minutes, if desired.

THE CLEVER COOK COULD:
- Substitute 1 cup smoked Gouda for the Cheddar cheese.
- Substitute ½ pound cooked, thinly sliced sausage for the bacon.
- Substitute challah or French bread for the ciabatta.
- Add ¾ cup sautéed mushrooms and caramelized onions instead of the peppers.

CITRUS POPOVER PANCAKE WITH MASCARPONE AND BERRIES

❄ SERVES 2 TO 4 ❄

Easier to make than individual pancakes, this giant pancake scented with lemon and orange makes a dazzling presentation. Like a popover, it magically puffs up into a light yet satisfying breakfast or brunch main course. Italian mascarpone cheese, spread on the hot pancake, melts into the surface, and powdered sugar sprinkled on the creamy cheese creates a light glaze. Accompany the pancake with grilled assorted sausages or crisp bacon for a hearty meal. You can also cut the pancake into wedges and serve it as a breakfast side dish.

INGREDIENTS:

¾ CUP MILK

½ CUP ALL-PURPOSE FLOUR

2 LARGE EGGS

2 TABLESPOONS GRANULATED SUGAR

1 TEASPOON VANILLA EXTRACT

1 TEASPOON FINELY CHOPPED LEMON ZEST

1 TEASPOON FINELY CHOPPED ORANGE ZEST

2 TABLESPOONS UNSALTED BUTTER

2 TABLESPOONS SOFTENED MASCARPONE CHEESE

2 CUPS SLICED FRESH STRAWBERRIES, OR ONE 12-OUNCE BAG FROZEN MIXED BERRIES, DEFROSTED, FOR SERVING

POWDERED SUGAR FOR GARNISH

1. Preheat the oven to 450°F. Combine the milk, flour, eggs, granulated sugar, vanilla, and citrus zests in a food processor fitted with the metal blade, a blender, or a medium bowl. Process or whisk until smooth.

2. Place the butter in a 10-inch pie plate or ovenproof skillet and put it in the oven for 3 minutes, or until the butter melts. Swirl the pan to coat it evenly with the melted butter.

3. Pour the batter into the pan and bake for 15 minutes. Reduce the heat to 350°F and bake for 15 more minutes, or until the pancake is nicely browned, cooked in the center, and well puffed. Slide onto a round platter, using a spatula. Spread with the mascarpone and top with the berries. Serve immediately, sprinkled generously with the powdered sugar.

THE CLEVER COOK COULD:

○ Double the recipe and bake in 2 pie plates.

○ Add 1 cup peeled and chopped pear or apple to the batter.

○ Serve the pancake as dessert.

CHOCOLATE-CHIP PECAN CRUMB COFFEE CAKE

❊ SERVES 10 TO 12 ❊

When I was growing up, my mom hosted Tuesday night card games. Among the sweets on our dining room table was a coffee cake with a rich layer of streusel. It was always the first to disappear. This moist cake, with a thick, crispy chocolate and pecan crumb topping, reminds me of that coffee cake. Serve it for breakfast or brunch, or as an afternoon snack with a cup of hot tea. On Christmas morning, present squares of the cake on a pretty holiday platter.

INGREDIENTS:

CRUMB TOPPING

1 CUP (2 STICKS) UNSALTED BUTTER AT ROOM TEMPERATURE, CUT INTO 1-INCH PIECES

1¼ CUPS PACKED DARK BROWN SUGAR

1 TABLESPOON PUMPKIN PIE SPICE

1½ CUPS ALL-PURPOSE FLOUR

1 CUP CHOPPED PECANS

1 CUP SEMISWEET CHOCOLATE CHIPS

———

CAKE

2¼ CUPS ALL-PURPOSE FLOUR

1 TEASPOON BAKING POWDER

1 TEASPOON BAKING SODA

½ TEASPOON SALT

2 TEASPOONS PUMPKIN PIE SPICE

½ CUP (1 STICK) UNSALTED BUTTER AT ROOM TEMPERATURE

¾ CUP PACKED DARK BROWN SUGAR

½ CUP GRANULATED SUGAR

3 LARGE EGGS

1¼ CUPS BUTTERMILK

1 TEASPOON VANILLA EXTRACT

1. Preheat the oven to 350°F. Butter and flour a 9-by-13-inch baking pan.

2. Make the topping: In a large bowl, combine the butter, brown sugar, and pumpkin pie spice. With 2 knives, cut in the butter. Add the flour and pecans and, using your fingers, blend the flour and butter together to make large crumblike pieces. Add the chocolate chips and quickly work them into the topping.

3. Make the cake: sift the flour, baking powder, baking soda, salt, and pumpkin pie spice onto a large sheet of waxed paper.

4. In a large mixing bowl, beat the butter with an electric mixer on medium speed until light and fluffy. Gradually add the sugars, continuing to beat until very light. Add the eggs one at a time, beating well after each addition. With the mixer on low speed, alternately beat in the flour mixture and the buttermilk, beating until the batter is just mixed. Add the vanilla and mix.

5. Spread the batter evenly in the prepared pan. Evenly sprinkle with the crumb topping, pressing it gently into the batter. Bake for 40 to 45 minutes, or until the top of the cake is firm and the streusel is crisp and bubbling. A skewer inserted into the center should come out clean. Let cool slightly in the pan on a wire rack. Serve warm, cut into squares.

ADVANCE PREPARATION:
Make up to 2 days ahead and keep in an airtight container at room temperature.

THE CLEVER COOK COULD:
○ Omit the chocolate chips in the topping and add 1 peeled, cored, and chopped apple or pear to the batter.
○ Substitute almonds or walnuts for the pecans in the topping.

BREAKFAST CROSTINI

❄ SERVES 4 TO 6 ❄

When you want a light bite with coffee, try these tasty toasts spread with slightly sweet mascarpone, topped with fruit, and drizzled with fragrant honey. Using toasted walnut or pecan bread adds extra texture and flavor. The crostini are perfect for a casual, easy breakfast since they take just a few minutes to assemble. I also like to serve them alongside scrambled eggs.

INGREDIENTS:

TWELVE ½-INCH-THICK SLICES FRENCH, WALNUT AND RAISIN, PECAN AND RAISIN, OR OTHER FAVORITE BREAD

¼ CUP MASCARPONE CHEESE

2 PEARS SUCH AS BOSC, COMICE, OR ANJOU, PEELED, CORED, AND THINLY SLICED

¼ CUP HONEY SUCH AS ORANGE BLOSSOM, WHITE TRUFFLE, OR LAVENDER

1. If the bread slices are large, cut them in half. Toast the slices until light brown. Let cool.

2. Place the toasts on a platter and spread each with about 1 teaspoon mascarpone. Arrange a few pear slices on top and drizzle with honey. Serve immediately.

ADVANCE PREPARATION:
Make up to 1 hour ahead, cover, and keep at room temperature.

THE CLEVER COOK COULD:

○ Garnish the crostini with pomegranate seeds.

○ Use sliced fresh figs, apples, or peeled Fuyu persimmons in place of the pears.

○ Serve the crostini as a first course, substituting soft unsalted butter for the mascarpone and topping them with sliced figs, sliced prosciutto, and shaved Parmesan cheese.

○ Serve the crostini as a dessert course, replacing the mascarpone with softened blue cheese or other triple cream cheese.

SCRAMBLED EGGS WITH CARAMELIZED ONIONS, SMOKED SALMON, AND HERBED CREAM CHEESE

❉ SERVES 4 TO 6 ❉

Straining the eggs ensures that they will be creamy when scrambled. Serve the eggs with Potato Pancake Frittata (page 183), warm squares of Chocolate-Chip Pecan Crumb Coffee Cake (page 94), a platter of fresh fruit, and a pitcher of White Wine Fruit Spritzer (page 49). If you're cooking for a crowd, this recipe doubles or triples well. You will need to use a much larger, deeper skillet to accommodate all of the ingredients.

INGREDIENTS:

3 TABLESPOONS UNSALTED BUTTER

1 TABLESPOON OLIVE OIL

1 LARGE ONION, FINELY CHOPPED

SALT AND FRESHLY GROUND BLACK PEPPER

12 LARGE EGGS

¼ CUP HERBED CREAM CHEESE

¼ POUND SMOKED SALMON, DICED

1 TABLESPOON FINELY CHOPPED FRESH PARSLEY FOR GARNISH

1. In a medium skillet, melt 2 tablespoons of the butter with the oil over medium heat. Sauté the onion for 12 minutes, or until golden brown and very tender. Season with salt and pepper.

2. In a medium bowl, whisk the eggs well to combine. Put a fine-mesh strainer over another bowl and strain the eggs, making sure that the albumen (the white stringy part) remains in the strainer. Season with salt and pepper and stir to combine.

3. In a deep medium skillet, melt the remaining 1 tablespoon butter over medium heat. Add the eggs and stir continuously with a wooden spoon. When the eggs begin to form curds, stir for 3 minutes more, or until the eggs are very creamy. Add the onion, cream cheese, and salmon, and cook for 2 to 3 minutes, or until the desired consistency. Do not let the eggs become dry. Turn into a shallow bowl and garnish with the parsley. Serve immediately.

ADVANCE PREPARATION:
Make up to 1 day ahead through step 1, cover, and refrigerate. Remove the onions from the refrigerator 1 hour before continuing.

PASTA FRITTATA

❄ SERVES 6 ❄

The first time I ever tasted pasta with eggs was at a breakfast spot that featured all sorts of unusual egg combinations. I thought it was a great way to use leftover pasta. If you don't have cooked spaghetti on hand, it can be boiled in just minutes. I use about ⅓ pound spaghetti, broken in half, to equal 2½ cups cooked. The frittata makes a wonderful weekend brunch dish or a Sunday supper accompanied by Two-Endive Salad with Pear, Walnuts, and Blue Cheese (page 79).

INGREDIENTS:

8 LARGE EGGS

¾ CUP GRATED SHARP CHEDDAR, COMTÉ, OR JACK CHEESE

SALT AND FRESHLY GROUND BLACK PEPPER

2 TABLESPOONS OLIVE OIL

3 ZUCCHINI, THINLY SLICED

3 GARLIC CLOVES, MINCED

2½ CUPS COOKED THIN SPAGHETTI

¼ CUP THINLY SLICED, WELL-DRAINED, SUN-DRIED TOMATOES PACKED IN OIL

½ CUP RICOTTA CHEESE

1. Preheat the oven to 350°F. In a medium bowl, whisk together the eggs, cheese, and salt and pepper to taste until the eggs are frothy.

2. In an ovenproof skillet large enough to hold the zucchini in one layer, heat the oil over medium-high heat. Sauté the zucchini, turning with tongs, for 5 to 6 minutes, or until golden on both sides. Add the garlic, pasta, and tomatoes and cook for 2 minutes, or until the garlic is fragrant and the pasta is well blended.

3. Add the egg mixture and evenly distribute the vegetables and the pasta. Reduce the heat to medium-low and cook, stirring occasionally, for 7 minutes, or until the bottom is lightly set. Arrange spoonfuls of the ricotta evenly on top of the frittata. Place in the oven and bake for 10 to 15 minutes, or until the frittata is puffed and brown. Let cool slightly. Serve hot or at room temperature, cut into wedges.

ADVANCE PREPARATION:
Make 2 hours ahead and keep at room temperature.

THE CLEVER COOK COULD:
○ Cut the frittata into small squares, top them with a dollop of sun-dried tomato or basil pesto, and serve as an appetizer.
○ Omit the pasta and add 2 eggs to make a lighter version.

SPICY JALAPEÑO CORNBREAD

❄ SERVES 12 TO 16 ❄

I seldom use canned ingredients, except for tomatoes, but canned cream corn adds moisture and appealing texture to this homey and very substantial cornbread. Canned diced jalapeño chiles are a practical alternative to fresh chiles. Look for a 4-ounce can, drain the chiles well, and add (to taste) to the batter.

INGREDIENTS:

1 CUP ALL-PURPOSE FLOUR

1 CUP YELLOW CORNMEAL

2 TEASPOONS BAKING POWDER

1 TEASPOON SALT

2 TABLESPOONS CANOLA OIL, PLUS ½ CUP

4 LEEKS, LIGHT GREEN AND WHITE PARTS ONLY, CLEANED AND FINELY CHOPPED

4 LARGE EGGS

2 CUPS SOUR CREAM

¾ POUND SHARP CHEDDAR CHEESE, SHREDDED

ONE 14¾-OUNCE CAN CREAMED CORN

2 TO 4 JALAPEÑO CHILES, SEEDED AND FINELY CHOPPED

1. Preheat the oven to 350°F. Butter a 9-by-13-inch baking pan. In a medium bowl, whisk the flour, cornmeal, baking powder, and salt.

2. In a large skillet, heat the 2 tablespoons oil over medium-high heat. Sauté the leeks for 7 to 10 minutes, or until softened and lightly caramelized.

3. In a large bowl, whisk the eggs together. Add the sour cream, the ½ cup oil, all but ½ cup of the shredded cheese, and the creamed corn. Whisk together until completely blended. Add the dry ingredients and mix until completely blended. Add the cooled leeks and the jalapeños to taste and mix until blended.

4. Pour the batter into the prepared pan and sprinkle with the remaining cheese. Bake for 50 to

60 minutes, or until a skewer inserted into the center comes out almost clean. Let cool slightly. Serve warm, cut into squares.

ADVANCE PREPARATION:
Make up to 2 days ahead, cover, and keep at room temperature. Reheat in a 350°F oven for about 20 minutes.

THE CLEVER COOK COULD:
- Slice and toast the cornbread and use as a base for creamy scrambled eggs.
- Cut into 1½-inch squares, top with sour cream, diced avocado, and tomato salsa, and serve as an appetizer.
- Serve with Turkey and Pinto Bean Chili (page 124): Cut the bread into large squares and then cut each square in half horizontally. Place each bottom half in a bowl, spoon the chili and condiments over the bread, and top with the top half.

MAIN COURSES

POULTRY

CHICKEN PAILLARDS WITH CRANBERRY-PORT SAUCE

❧ SERVES 4 TO 6 ☙

If you want to put together a holiday meal for a small group in just a few minutes, this is the recipe to make. Chicken paillards lend themselves to last-minute preparation with a minimum of fuss. The cranberry-port sauce enlivens the chicken with holiday flavors. Serve the chicken with Yam and Winter Squash Purée (page 178) and Braised Spinach with Crispy Shallots (page 175) for a memorable meal.

❧ **RECOMMENDED WINE:**
The combination of sweet and tart calls for a smooth Pinot Noir or for this season's Nouveau red. An off-dry rosé or Chenin Blanc will also make a surprisingly delightful match.

INGREDIENTS:

SIX 6-OUNCE BONED, SKINLESS CHICKEN BREAST HALVES

SERIOUSLY SIMPLE SEASONING SALT (PAGE 208)

FRESHLY GROUND BLACK PEPPER

OLIVE OIL SPRAY

¾ CUP CHICKEN BROTH

3 TABLESPOONS TAWNY PORT

½ CUP FRESH CRANBERRY SAUCE OR CRANBERRY-POMEGRANATE SAUCE WITH SATSUMAS (PAGE 212)

2 TABLESPOONS FINELY CHOPPED FRESH PARSLEY FOR GARNISH

1. Place each breast half between 2 pieces of plastic wrap and use a mallet or the bottom of a saucepan to pound to an even thickness of ⅛ inch. Season with salt and pepper.

2. Coat a large nonstick skillet with olive oil spray and place over medium-high heat. Sauté the chicken, in batches if necessary, for 2 to 3 minutes per side, or until no pinkness remains. Remove to a platter, overlapping the paillards for a pretty presentation. Cover with aluminum foil and keep warm.

3. Add the broth and port to the pan and deglaze over medium-high heat by scraping up the brown bits. Add the cranberry sauce and whisk for 2 minutes, or until the sauce is slightly reduced and has a glazelike consistency. Spoon the sauce over the paillards, garnish with parsley, and serve immediately.

ADVANCE PREPARATION:
Make up to 4 hours ahead through step 1, cover, and refrigerate.

MEDITERRANEAN-STYLE CHICKEN WITH CAPERS, PLUMS, AND OLIVES

SERVES 4 TO 6

Adapted from *The Silver Palate Cookbook*'s Chicken Marbella, this sweet and savory chicken can be served hot right out of the oven, at room temperature, or chilled for a luncheon buffet. You can easily double or triple the recipe for a crowd. Accompany with Green Beans with Caramelized Red Onion and Mushroom Topping (page 180).

RECOMMENDED WINE:

The versatility of this dish is paralleled by the flexibility of wine choices. Aromatic whites such as Viognier or Sauvignon Blanc mirror the recipe's herbs and fruit. A softer, fruit-driven red will perform likewise: select a southern French Rhône, California or Australian Syrah, or Spanish Tempranillo or Garnacha (Grenache). It's hard to make a mistake!

INGREDIENTS:

MARINADE

15 SMALL GARLIC CLOVES, PEELED

2 TABLESPOONS DRIED OREGANO

SERIOUSLY SIMPLE SEASONING SALT (PAGE 208)

FRESHLY GROUND BLACK PEPPER

⅓ CUP RED WINE VINEGAR

⅓ CUP OLIVE OIL

1 LEEK, WHITE AND LIGHT GREEN PARTS ONLY, CLEANED AND FINELY CHOPPED

½ CUP DRIED WHOLE PITTED APRICOTS

¾ CUP DRIED WHOLE PITTED PLUMS

⅓ CUP PITTED GREEN OLIVES

⅓ CUP PITTED KALAMATA OLIVES

⅓ CUP CAPERS WITH SOME BRINE

_____

TWO 3- TO 3½-POUND CHICKENS, CUT INTO SERVING PIECES

2 TABLESPOONS PACKED BROWN SUGAR

¾ CUP DRY RED WINE SUCH AS ZINFANDEL OR SYRAH

2 TABLESPOONS FINELY CHOPPED FRESH PARSLEY OR CILANTRO FOR GARNISH

1. Make the marinade: in a bowl, stir together the garlic, oregano, salt and pepper to taste, vinegar, oil, leek, apricots, plums, olives, and capers until blended.

2. Place the chicken in a lock-top plastic bag and pour in the marinade. Turn the chicken pieces in the bag to coat them evenly. Seal the bag and refrigerate for 2 to 4 hours.

3. Preheat the oven to 425°F. Place the chicken in baking pans in a single layer. Arrange the marinade ingredients around the chicken. In a small bowl, dissolve the brown sugar in the wine, stirring to blend. Pour over the chicken.

4. Roast the chicken, basting once or twice, for 40 to 45 minutes, or until the chicken is nicely browned and cooked through, and no pink color remains.

5. To serve, arrange the chicken pieces with the fruit and olives on a platter and top with some of the pan juices. Garnish with the parsley and serve immediately.

ADVANCE PREPARATION:
Make up to 4 hours ahead through step 1, cover, and refrigerate. Or make 1 day ahead and serve cold or at room temperature.

CITRUS-GLAZED CHICKEN WITH ARTICHOKE HEARTS AND THYME

❧ SERVES 4 TO 6 ❧

I am always searching for chicken recipes that can become standbys for last minute entertaining. My friend Denny Luria suggested this easy, rustic dish. The garlic cloves and lemon and orange slices become slightly caramelized, and the artichoke hearts complement the citrus. Serve with a simple rice pilaf and Braised Spinach with Crispy Shallots (page 175).

❧ RECOMMENDED WINE:

The tartness of citrus and artichokes often poses a challenge for wine. The solution is actually very easy—simply uncork a wine with good natural acidity, such as a fresh, clean Pinot Gris or Sauvignon Blanc. If you prefer red, a young, fruity Sangiovese or Chianti will captivate the senses.

INGREDIENTS:
MARINADE
GRATED ZEST AND JUICE (ABOUT ½ CUP) FROM 1 ORANGE

GRATED ZEST AND JUICE (ABOUT 2 TABLESPOONS) FROM 1 MEYER OR OTHER LEMON

1 TEASPOON BALSAMIC GLAZE (PAGE 209), OR 2 TEASPOONS BALSAMIC VINEGAR

3 TABLESPOONS OLIVE OIL

2 TEASPOONS FINELY CHOPPED FRESH THYME, OR 1 TEASPOON DRIED THYME

1 TEASPOON SERIOUSLY SIMPLE SEASONING SALT (PAGE 208)

FRESHLY GROUND BLACK PEPPER

12 GARLIC CLOVES, PEELED

1 LEEK, LIGHT GREEN AND WHITE PARTS ONLY, CLEANED AND FINELY CHOPPED

———

ONE 4-POUND CHICKEN, CUT INTO SERVING PIECES

1 ORANGE, ENDS TRIMMED, CUT CROSSWISE INTO ½-INCH SLICES, AND EACH SLICE CUT INTO HALF-MOONS

1 MEYER OR OTHER LEMON, ENDS TRIMMED AND CUT CROSSWISE INTO ½-INCH SLICES

ONE 8-OUNCE PACKAGE FROZEN ARTICHOKE HEARTS, DEFROSTED

BALSAMIC GLAZE (PAGE 209) AS NEEDED

THYME SPRIGS FOR GARNISH (OPTIONAL)

1. Make the marinade: In a bowl, stir together the citrus zest and juice, balsamic glaze, and oil until blended. Add the thyme, salt, pepper to taste, garlic, and leek. Taste and adjust the seasonings.

2. Place the chicken in a lock-top plastic bag and pour in the marinade. Turn the chicken pieces

in the bag to coat them evenly. Seal the bag and refrigerate for 30 minutes to 4 hours.

3. Preheat the oven to 425°F. Place the chicken and marinade in a large, shallow roasting pan. Arrange the citrus slices around the chicken and coat with some of the marinade.

4. Roast for 30 minutes. Baste the chicken pieces. Scatter the artichoke hearts around the chicken and baste. Roast for 25 to 30 more minutes, or until the chicken skin is brown and crispy, and the chicken is cooked through. Taste the sauce and adjust with balsamic glaze, if desired.

5. Serve directly from the roasting pan or place on a platter and garnish with the thyme sprigs, if desired. Serve immediately.

ADVANCE PREPARATION:
Make up to 4 hours ahead through step 1, cover, and refrigerate.

CORNISH HENS WITH BRAISED CABBAGE AND APPLE

SERVES 4 TO 6

Cornish hens sparkle in this recipe and offer a welcome change from chicken. I like to serve them to a small group for a holiday dinner party. The marinated hens become brown, crispy, and very moist as they roast. The cabbage softens and acquires a slight sweetness from the apple. Accompany with Braised Spinach with Crispy Shallots (page 175). For dessert, try Chocolate-Peppermint Pudding Cakes with Peppermint Stick Ice Cream (page 205).

RECOMMENDED WINE:

The richness, smokiness, and sweetness of this recipe will pair marvelously with a full-bodied, barrel-fermented Chardonnay. A Riesling's fresh fruit will contrast beautifully with the cabbage and bacon, and at the same time resonate with the apple. Finally, a lush, smoky oak-spiced Pinot Noir will match the dish's body and savoriness stride for stride.

INGREDIENTS:
MARINADE

1 TABLESPOON SOY SAUCE

2 TABLESPOONS APPLE BRANDY

¼ CUP OLIVE OIL

2 SHALLOTS, FINELY CHOPPED

1 TEASPOON FINELY CHOPPED FRESH THYME, OR ½ TEASPOON DRIED THYME

1 TEASPOON SERIOUSLY SIMPLE SEASONING SALT (PAGE 208)

FRESHLY GROUND BLACK PEPPER

———

THREE 1½-POUND CORNISH HENS, HALVED

6 STRIPS THICK-CUT BACON, CUT INTO 2-INCH PIECES

2 TABLESPOONS UNSALTED BUTTER

1 ONION, FINELY CHOPPED

ONE 1½-POUND GREEN CABBAGE, CORED AND COARSELY CHOPPED

1 LARGE PIPPIN OR GRANNY SMITH APPLE, PEELED, CORED, AND COARSELY CHOPPED

½ CUP APPLE BRANDY

SALT AND FRESHLY GROUND BLACK PEPPER

¼ CUP HEAVY CREAM OR CRÈME FRAÎCHE (OPTIONAL)

3 TABLESPOONS FINELY CHOPPED FRESH PARSLEY FOR GARNISH

1 BUNCH WATERCRESS, THICK STEMS REMOVED, FOR GARNISH

1. Make the marinade: In a small bowl, stir together the soy sauce, brandy, oil, shallots, thyme, salt, and pepper to taste. Place the hens in a lock-top plastic bag and pour in the marinade. Turn the hens in the bag to coat them evenly. Seal the bag and refrigerate for 2 to 8 hours.

2. Preheat the oven to 425°F. Place the hens breast-side up on a baking sheet. Pour the marinade over the hens. Roast for 40 to 45 minutes, basting with the pan juices every

15 minutes, or until the hens are golden brown. Loosely cover with aluminum foil to keep warm.

3. While the hens are roasting, in a large Dutch oven over medium-high heat, brown the bacon, turning with tongs, for about 4 minutes, or until crisp. Remove to paper towels to drain. Drain off all but 1 tablespoon of the bacon drippings, place the pot over medium heat, and melt the butter. Sauté the onion for 5 to 7 minutes, or until softened and lightly browned, stirring to scrape up the brown bits. Add the cabbage and apple, stir a few times, cover, and cook for about 10 minutes, or until the mixture

is softened but still retains some texture. Add the apple brandy, salt and pepper to taste, and the cream, if using. Raise the heat to high and cook for 2 minutes, or until the alcohol has evaporated and the sauce is slightly reduced. Taste and adjust the seasonings.

4. To serve, spoon the cabbage mixture on a platter and arrange the hens on top. Drizzle with the pan juices, garnish with the parsley and watercress, and serve immediately.

ADVANCE PREPARATION:
Make the marinade and cabbage up to 1 day ahead, cover, and refrigerate. Bring the cabbage to room temperature before reheating.

THE CLEVER COOK COULD:
- Serve the hens and cabbage on individual plates, garnishing each portion with watercress sprigs.
- Serve the cabbage as a bed for Roast Duck Legs with Caramelized Shallots and Garlic (page 127) or any roast pork dish.
- Serve the hens chilled on their own for a buffet lunch.

ROAST TURKEY WITH MAPLE-BALSAMIC BUTTER RUB

SERVES 10 TO 14

The key to seasoning the turkey with this butter rub is to blot the bird dry, which enables the rub to adhere to the skin. You can also stuff the turkey, but it takes about an hour longer to cook. An instant-read thermometer is a must for ensuring a perfectly cooked bird. Remember that the internal temperature will increase by a few degrees once the turkey is removed from the oven. Serve with Make-Ahead Turkey Gravy (page 216). Strain the pan drippings for making the gravy, and use a fat separator to remove the fat from the strained drippings.

RECOMMENDED WINE:

The underrated Riesling is magic with the sweet and savory tastes in this turkey recipe. Lighter reds such as Beaujolais Nouveau, Grenache, Pinot Noir, and Côtes du Rhône are also excellent choices.

INGREDIENTS:

ONE 14- TO 16-POUND TURKEY, PATTED DRY

───────

RUB

2 SHALLOTS, FINELY CHOPPED

3 TABLESPOONS PURE MAPLE SYRUP

1 TABLESPOON BALSAMIC GLAZE (PAGE 209)

1 TABLESPOON SOY SAUCE

2 TABLESPOONS CHOPPED FRESH THYME, OR 2 TEASPOONS DRIED THYME

1 TABLESPOON SERIOUSLY SIMPLE SEASONING SALT (PAGE 208)

½ CUP (1 STICK) UNSALTED BUTTER AT ROOM TEMPERATURE

───────

1 LARGE ORANGE, PEEL INTACT AND SLICED CROSSWISE

3 ONIONS; 1 SLICED, 2 COARSELY CHOPPED

2 CARROTS, PEELED AND SLICED

2 CUPS EASY TURKEY STOCK (PAGE 217) OR CHICKEN BROTH, OR MORE IF NEEDED

1. Remove the turkey from the refrigerator 1 hour before roasting.

2. Make the rub: In a small bowl, stir together all of the ingredients until well blended. Taste and adjust the seasonings.

3. Preheat the oven to 425°F. Place the turkey on a piece of aluminum foil on the counter. Starting around the main body cavity, carefully slip your fingers under the skin and loosen the skin, being careful not to break the skin. (You may need to wear rubber gloves if you have long fingernails.) Pat the rub under the skin and then pat it all over the bird on top of the skin. (If some of the rub falls off, that is okay; it will flavor the gravy.)

4. Place the orange and onion slices in the cavity. Insert a wooden skewer through the thighs to hold the drumsticks together. Place the chopped onions and the carrots on the bottom of a large roasting pan. Pour the 2 cups stock over the vegetables. Set a nonstick roasting rack in the roasting pan and place the turkey breast-side up on the rack.

5. Roast in the center of the oven for 20 minutes. Reduce the oven temperature to 325°F and roast, basting about every 45 minutes with the pan juices, until a thermometer inserted into the thickest part of a thigh away from the bone registers 170°F and the juices run clear. You may need to add more stock if the pan becomes too dry.

If the bird becomes too dark, tent a piece of aluminum foil on top. A 16-pound turkey should take about 4 hours. Be sure to check the temperature at 30-minute intervals as the finish time approaches.

6. Transfer the turkey to a large platter or carving board. Let rest for at least 20 minutes before carving. Discard the vegetables.

ADVANCE PREPARATION:
Make the rub 2 days ahead, cover, and refrigerate. Remove both the turkey and the rub from the refrigerator 1 hour before roasting.

THE CLEVER COOK COULD:
- Stuff the turkey: Omit the onion and orange. Use your favorite stuffing. Loosely stuff the turkey in the neck and main cavities. Close the flaps with wooden skewers. A stuffed 16-pound bird should take about 5 hours to cook.
- Use the rub on a 3½- to 4-pound chicken and roast for about 1 hour at 425°F.

THANKSGIVING TIPS

———

For some cooks, pulling off a Thanksgiving dinner can be a daunting task. But recognizing that it is important to keep traditions alive, I've spent years perfecting advance preparations for this important meal. I knew that the more things I did in advance, the more enjoyable—and Seriously Simple—the holiday could be. Now, I just print out my list from the computer, knowing that it can be adjusted each year.

On the following pages, you'll find a guide to help make the planning and cooking simple for you, so your Thanksgiving dinner comes off with ease. No matter how simple you keep things, you still must make lists, shop in advance, and have a schedule. You don't necessarily need pressed linen napkins and fine china for a memorable meal. The key ingredients to a successful Thanksgiving are good food and some planning. Vary the menu with your personal favorites.

❖ ❖ ❖

Seriously Simple Thanksgiving Menu

Spicy Sausage and Chicken Liver Pâté, PAGE 52

Roast Turkey with Maple-Balsamic Butter Rub, PAGE 112,
and Make-Ahead Turkey Gravy, PAGE 216

Sausage, Dried Fruit, and Nut Stuffing, PAGE 187

Cranberry-Pomegranate Sauce with Satsumas, PAGE 212

Orange Cranberry Sauce, PAGE 213

Perfect Mashed Potatoes, PAGE 185

Yam and Winter Squash Purée, PAGE 178

Green Beans with Caramelized Red Onion and
Mushroom Topping, PAGE 180

Pumpkin-Caramel Ice Cream Pie, PAGE 195
with warm Caramel Sauce, PAGE 218

Double-Persimmon Pudding, PAGE 193

Thanksgiving Planning Countdown

———

The menu on the previous page looks long, but I don't expect that you'll make the entire meal yourself. Thanksgiving dinner is often a potluck affair, so pick and choose which foods you'd like to prepare, and ask guests to bring other items. This countdown includes everything—eliminate any steps that are irrelevant.

1 MONTH BEFORE:
- Prepare Spicy Sausage and Chicken Liver Pâté and freeze.
- Make Easy Turkey Stock and freeze in small containers.
- Make Pumpkin-Caramel Ice Cream Pie and freeze.

2 WEEKS BEFORE:
- Plan your menu.

1 WEEK BEFORE:
- Order a fresh turkey: To ensure ample servings for dinner, as well as leftovers the next day, allow ¾ to 1 pound per person.
- Plan your table setting and decorations.
- Make your grocery shopping lists, separating staples from fresh foods.
- Begin shopping for staples.
- Shop for any Essential Holiday Equipment (see page 28).

SATURDAY BEFORE:
- Make Caramel Sauce for pie.
- Choose dishes, glassware, tablecloths and napkins, serving dishes, and serving utensils.
- Sharpen carving knife.

MONDAY:
- Complete shopping lists.
- Begin shopping for produce and other fresh food.
- Organize refrigerator, cleaning out to make extra room for turkey.
- Defrost turkey stock.

TUESDAY:
- Gently reheat stock and make gravy.
- Make Orange-Cranberry Sauce and/or Cranberry-Pomegranate Sauce and refrigerate in large glass jars.
- Prepare vegetables for stuffing, place in lock-top plastic bags, and refrigerate.
- Clean and chop parsley, place in lock-top plastic bags, and refrigerate.

Remove chicken liver pâté from freezer and place in refrigerator to defrost.

WEDNESDAY:
- Pick up turkey and fresh herbs and refrigerate.
- Make Yam and Winter Squash Purée and refrigerate.
- Clean green beans and make topping. Refrigerate in lock-top plastic bags.
- Buy flowers and arrange, if needed.
- Chill wines and water.
- Set the table and buffet, arranging serving pieces, platters, and trivets. You can even stick a Post-it on each platter designating which dish will go in each piece.
- Organize coffee and tea.
- Plan a schedule for the next day, determining what time the turkey must be put in the oven (allowing the oven to preheat).

THANKSGIVING DAY:
- Make Double-Persimmon Pudding.
- Put turkey in oven (see chart at right).
- If stuffing is not in turkey, place in a casserole and bake for 45 minutes before serving.
- Make Perfect Mashed Potatoes and keep warm in a double boiler.
- Arrange the bar.
- Reheat gravy and add drippings from turkey.
- Reheat Yam and Winter Squash Purée.
- Assemble green beans and topping.
- Fill water glasses and wineglasses.
- Put out pâté with water crackers and crudités.
- Carve turkey.
- Defrost pie 30 minutes before serving and reheat Caramel Sauce.
- Reheat persimmon pudding 15 minutes before serving.

APPROXIMATE ROASTING TIMES FOR AN UNSTUFFED TURKEY ROASTED AT 325°F:
Use this only as a guide to help budget your time, keeping in mind that the doneness of an unstuffed turkey should always be judged by its internal temperature rather than just by the clock. Times also vary depending on the oven temperature. Loosely cover the bird with aluminum foil if it gets too brown to avoid burning the skin.

8 TO 12 POUNDS:	2¾ TO 3 HOURS
12 TO 14 POUNDS:	3 TO 3¾ HOURS
14 TO 18 POUNDS:	3¾ TO 4¼ HOURS
18 TO 20 POUNDS:	4¼ TO 4½ HOURS
20 TO 24 POUNDS:	4½ TO 5 HOURS

When testing for doneness, insert an instant-read thermometer into the innermost part of the thigh without touching the bone. When the internal temperature reads 170°F, remove the turkey from the oven and cover it loosely with aluminum foil. The bird will continue to cook while resting for 20 minutes, allowing you time to finish the gravy and to prepare to carve. The internal temperature will rise to about 175°F.

Thanksgiving Wine Advice

BY PETER MARKS

Of all Thanksgiving preparations, selecting wine often draws the most fear. This is the time of year when wine pundits gush forth all sorts of advice on what to serve with the turkey and all the trimmings.

The most important advice is, Don't fret. Over the years the most important Thanksgiving wine lesson I've learned is to serve wines you like and you know your guests will like. How do you accomplish this task? Easy . . . serve a variety.

The Thanksgiving feast offers a variety of flavors, textures, and sweetness levels, from Aunt Linda's homemade cranberry sauce to Uncle Jake's sautéed Brussels sprouts. Often, the roasted bird plays a background role. Two important points to keep in mind: One, with all these foods on your plate, you need a flavorful wine with good intensity to stand up to the culinary competition. Second, tasting salty, savory, spicy, and sweet flavors all at once calls for an assortment of wines ranging from dry to sweet.

More specifically, enjoy aromatic whites such as Chardonnay (make sure it is rich and buttery), Gewürztraminer and Riesling (dry or sweet), and Viognier. Fruit-forward reds such as Gamay (Beaujolais, especially the Nouveau), Pinot Noir, Syrah, and Zinfandel will all make a successful marriage on the table.

PLUM-GLAZED TURKEY BREAST WITH SAKE AND PEAR SAUCE

SERVES 6 TO 8

My friend Perla Muhlstein came up with this idea, which I have embellished with a few of my own flavor components. I can prepare the recipe in just minutes on a busy weekday. The best part is that pan juices form a sauce while the turkey breast roasts. The recipe is a good addition to your holiday table if you want extra turkey the next day. Serve with Green Beans with Caramelized Red Onion and Mushroom Topping (page 180) and baby roast potatoes.

RECOMMENDED WINE:
Pinot Noir and Gewürztraminer are perfect partners with the traditional Thanksgiving meal, and especially with this turkey dish where the fruits and Asian spices echo the flavors in the wines.

INGREDIENTS:
MARINADE
¼ CUP CHINESE PLUM SAUCE

¼ CUP SAKE

1 TABLESPOON GRATED FRESH GINGER

1 LEEK, WHITE AND LIGHT GREEN PARTS ONLY, CLEANED AND FINELY CHOPPED

1 PEAR SUCH AS COMICE OR ANJOU, PEELED, CORED, AND CHOPPED

SALT AND FRESHLY GROUND BLACK PEPPER

———

ONE 3½-POUND BONED AND TIED TURKEY BREAST

1 TABLESPOON CHINESE PLUM SAUCE

2 TABLESPOONS FINELY CHOPPED FRESH PARSLEY FOR GARNISH

1. Make the marinade: in a small bowl, stir together all of the ingredients, including salt and pepper to taste.

2. Place the turkey breast in a large lock-top plastic bag and pour in the marinade. Turn the turkey in the bag to coat it evenly. Seal the bag and refrigerate for 3 to 4 hours. (If you don't have time, go directly to step 3 and pour the marinade over the turkey.)

3. Preheat the oven to 375°F. Place the turkey in a roasting pan. Pour the marinade over the turkey. Cover the pan tightly with aluminum foil. Roast for 1½ to 2 hours, or until the internal temperature is 155°F.

continued on next page

4. Raise the oven temperature to 425°F. Remove the foil. Brush the turkey with the plum sauce and roast for about 20 more minutes, or until an instant-read thermometer inserted into the thickest part of the breast registers 160°F, basting with the pan juices halfway through the cooking time. The skin should turn a deep brown color.

5. Place the turkey on a carving board and reserve the sauce in the roasting pan. Cover the turkey with aluminum foil and let rest for 15 to 20 minutes before carving. Cut the turkey into ½-inch-thick slices and overlap them on a serving platter. Spoon the sauce over the turkey and garnish with the parsley.

ADVANCE PREPARATION:
Make 4 hours ahead through step 1 and refrigerate.

THE CLEVER COOK COULD:
○ Use leftover turkey in a salad with spinach, pears, and toasted pecans, adding any remaining sauce to a basic vinaigrette.
○ Cut the turkey into 1-inch pieces and add to your favorite stir-fry.
○ Use leftover slices of the turkey for sandwiches and add a bit of the sauce to mayonnaise for spreading on the bread.

TURKEY WITH ORANGE-HERB BASTING SAUCE

❧ SERVES 6 TO 10 ☙

My friend Janice Wald Henderson describes this as her no-fail turkey recipe, and after trying it I couldn't agree more. The sauce is easy to prepare, and the best part for those of us who are carving challenged is that the pieces are already cut up, except for the breast. Serve with Perfect Mashed Potatoes (page 185) and Roasted Brussels Sprouts (page 177).

❧ **RECOMMENDED WINE:**

The orange and herb flavors call for a fresh, unoaked Chardonnay or Viognier, or a young, zesty Riesling (dry to slightly sweet). If a red is required, try a soft, bright, youthful Grenache.

INGREDIENTS:
BASTING SAUCE
ONE 6-OUNCE CAN FROZEN ORANGE JUICE CONCENTRATE

¼ CUP ORANGE LIQUEUR SUCH AS COINTREAU

4 TABLESPOONS UNSALTED BUTTER AT ROOM TEMPERATURE

2 TABLESPOONS FINELY CHOPPED FRESH HERBS SUCH AS PARSLEY, SAGE, AND THYME

SERIOUSLY SIMPLE SEASONING SALT (PAGE 208)

FRESHLY GROUND BLACK PEPPER

———

ONE 3-POUND WHOLE TURKEY BREAST

TWO 1-POUND TURKEY THIGHS

TWO 1-POUND TURKEY DRUMSTICKS

SERIOUSLY SIMPLE SEASONING SALT (PAGE 208)

1½ TO 2 CUPS CHICKEN BROTH OR EASY TURKEY STOCK (PAGE 217)

ORANGE SLICES AND PARSLEY OR WATERCRESS FOR GARNISH

1. Make the basting sauce: In a glass measuring cup, combine the orange juice concentrate, liqueur, and butter and microwave for 1 minute, or until all of the ingredients are liquid. Or heat in a small saucepan over medium heat. Stir in the herbs and salt and pepper to taste.

2. Preheat the oven to 325°F. Arrange the turkey parts in a shallow roasting pan, placing the breast skin-side up. Pour the basting sauce over the turkey and turn each piece with tongs to coat it evenly. Sprinkle a little salt on each piece. Pour ½ cup of the broth around the pan.

3. Roast, basting every 15 minutes and turning the legs, until the pieces are cooked through, brown, and crispy. You will need to add more broth as the pan gets brown and dry, so watch carefully. Total cooking time is 1 ¾ to 2 ¼ hours. The breast may be done sooner. It should read 160°F on an instant-read thermometer. The dark-meat parts should register 175°F.

continued on next page

. . . continued

4. Transfer the turkey breast to a carving board and let rest for at least 15 minutes. Arrange the other pieces on a platter. Carve the breast and arrange on the platter.

5. While the turkey is resting, place the roasting pan over medium-high heat, add 1 cup of the broth and deglaze the pan by scraping up the brown bits. Taste and adjust the seasonings. Pour over the turkey. Garnish the platter with orange slices and parsley. Serve immediately.

ADVANCE PREPARATION:
Make up to 1 hour ahead through step 3, loosely cover, and keep at room temperature.

THE CLEVER COOK COULD:
- Cut the turkey breast into 1½-inch chunks and make a salad with an orange vinaigrette.
- Add leftover turkey to a quick vegetable soup.
- Cut any leftover turkey into 1-inch pieces and use in a stir-fry.

TURKEY AND PINTO BEAN CHILI

SERVES 8 TO 12

This chili, reminiscent of a rich Mexican mole sauce, is packed with flavor. Start the meal with your favorite guacamole and chips and accompany with a variety of purchased fresh salsas; serve the chili with Spicy Jalapeño Cornbread (page 100). Ask your butcher to provide dark turkey ground for chili, which will give the finished dish extra texture. Measure all the ingredients ahead, so you can cook the chili quickly. If you are having a crowd, you can double the recipe. Make sure to use two large pots.

RECOMMENDED WINE:

Match the beans, chocolate, and spices with a velvety and fruity Merlot or Zinfandel. A sweetish Gewürztraminer or Muscat will also fit the bill. Very cold beer would be equally delicious.

INGREDIENTS:

4 TABLESPOONS CANOLA OIL

3 POUNDS CHILI-GROUND DARK-MEAT TURKEY

3 LARGE ONIONS, FINELY CHOPPED

8 GARLIC CLOVES, MINCED

1 TABLESPOON PLUS 1 TEASPOON DRIED OREGANO

1 TABLESPOON PLUS 1 TEASPOON GROUND CUMIN

2 TEASPOONS GROUND CORIANDER

1 TEASPOON GROUND CINNAMON

½ CUP CHILI POWDER

2 TO 3 TEASPOONS CHIPOTLE CHILE POWDER, OR ½ TO 1 CHOPPED CANNED CHIPOTLE CHILE IN ADOBO SAUCE

ONE 12-OUNCE CAN OR BOTTLE OF BEER

2½ CUPS WATER

ONE 28-OUNCE CAN CRUSHED TOMATOES

SALT AND FRESHLY GROUND BLACK PEPPER

1 CUP JARRED ROASTED RED AND YELLOW BELL PEPPERS, RINSED, DRAINED, AND FINELY CHOPPED

TWO 16-OUNCE CANS PINTO BEANS, RINSED AND DRAINED

½ OUNCE (½ SQUARE) UNSWEETENED CHOCOLATE, GRATED

———

CONDIMENTS

SOUR CREAM, TOMATO SALSA, AND GRATED SHARP CHEDDAR CHEESE

SLICED SCALLIONS OR CHOPPED RED ONIONS

FINELY CHOPPED, SEEDED JALAPEÑO CHILES

1. In a 6-quart pot, heat 2 tablespoons of the oil over medium-high heat. Sauté the turkey in batches for 5 to 7 minutes, or until well browned. Do not crowd the pan or the meat will steam. Remove to a bowl.

2. Add the remaining 2 tablespoons of the oil to the pot and sauté the onions for 5 to 7 minutes, or until soft and lightly browned. In a small bowl, combine the garlic, oregano, cumin, coriander, cinnamon, and chili powder. Sprinkle over the onions and sauté for 2 minutes, or until the spices release their aroma.

3. Add the beer, water, and tomatoes and bring to a low simmer. Return the meat to the pot. Season with salt and pepper and simmer, partially covered and stirring occasionally, for about 25 minutes, or until the meat is tender.

4. Add the peppers, beans, and chocolate and cook, partially covered, over medium heat for 15 more minutes, or until slightly thickened. Remove the cover the last 5 minutes of cooking to reduce the liquid. Taste and adjust the seasonings. Serve in chili or pottery bowls. Pass small bowls of the condiments at the table.

ADVANCE PREPARATION:
Make up to 3 days ahead, cover, and refrigerate. Remove from the refrigerator 1 hour before serving and reheat. The chile may be frozen up to 1 month ahead; defrost, reheat gently, and adjust the seasonings.

ROAST DUCK LEGS WITH CARAMELIZED SHALLOTS AND GARLIC

SERVES 8

Recipes don't get much easier than this one. And the result is simply delicious. The caramelized sweet garlic and shallots are a perfect counterpoint to the crisp duck legs. Cooking duck legs is so much easier than roasting a whole duck because you avoid carving. Just be sure to drain the legs after cooking, because they release a lot of fat. Serve the duck legs on a bed of Polenta with Butternut Squash and Chestnuts (page 182). They are also wonderful with Cranberry-Pomegranate Sauce with Satsumas (page 212) and Rice Pilaf with Dried Cherries and Toasted Pistachios (page 189). Roasted Brussels Sprouts (page 177) are another excellent accompaniment.

RECOMMENDED WINE:

These succulent duck legs demand a rich, bold red such as a Cabernet Sauvignon or Merlot. Pinot Noir also has the power to stand together with this wintertime dish.

INGREDIENTS:

EIGHT ¾- TO 1-POUND DUCK LEGS

SERIOUSLY SIMPLE SEASONING SALT (PAGE 208)

FRESHLY GROUND BLACK PEPPER

16 LARGE SHALLOTS

24 GARLIC CLOVES, PEELED

2 TABLESPOONS FINELY CHOPPED FRESH PARSLEY FOR GARNISH

1. Preheat the oven to 325°F. Place the duck legs on a large baking sheet and prick them with a fork to help release the fat during cooking. Season evenly with salt and pepper. Scatter the shallots and garlic around the pan.

2. Roast the duck legs for 1½ to 2 hours, or until all the fat has rendered and the legs are very crisp and cooked through. Toss the garlic and shallots with tongs occasionally so they cook evenly; when they are very brown and cooked through, after about 1¼ hours, remove to paper towels to drain.

3. When the duck legs are done, remove to paper towels to soak up any remaining fat. Place on a platter along with the garlic and shallots. Sprinkle with the parsley and serve immediately.

THE CLEVER COOK COULD:

° Shred the meat from the duck legs and add it to Winter Chopped Salad (page 80) instead of chicken.

° Use the duck fat instead of olive oil to roast potatoes in the oven.

° Serve the duck with the braised cabbage and apple from the Cornish hen recipe (page 110).

° Serve with Cranberry-Pomegranate Sauce (page 212) or Orange-Cranberry Sauce (page 213), or any purchased fruit relish.

MEATS

BRISKET WITH FIGS AND BUTTERNUT SQUASH

SERVES 6 TO 8

Make the brisket a day ahead because the meat is easier to cut into very thin slices after it has chilled. Winter squash and figs make a great autumn pairing. If the season for fresh figs is short, I use dried figs. The brisket and sauce are simple to prepare in advance. Just be sure to taste the sauce before serving and brighten the flavor with Balsamic Glaze, if necessary. I like to serve the brisket with Green Beans with Caramelized Red Onion and Mushroom Topping (page 180) and Noodle Kugel (page 174). If you are keeping kosher, serve with Roasted Potato Wedges with Leeks and Thyme (page 184) instead of the kugel.

RECOMMENDED WINE:

A simple wine and food pairing guideline is to serve the same type of wine that is used in the recipe. Thus, a rich and full-bodied Merlot or Cabernet Sauvignon will do the trick. Great kosher examples are available from Hagafen and Herzog.

INGREDIENTS:

ONE 4- TO 5-POUND FIRST-CUT BRISKET, PATTED DRY

SALT AND FRESHLY GROUND BLACK PEPPER

3 TABLESPOONS OLIVE OIL

4 ONIONS, THINLY SLICED

4 CARROTS, PEELED AND SLICED

ONE 1-POUND BAG PEELED, SEEDED, AND CUBED BUTTERNUT SQUASH, OR ONE 2-POUND BUTTERNUT SQUASH, PEELED, SEEDED, AND CUT INTO 2-INCH CUBES

8 GARLIC CLOVES, HALVED LENGTHWISE

1 TABLESPOON FINELY CHOPPED FRESH THYME, OR 1 TEASPOON DRIED THYME

1½ CUPS DRY RED WINE SUCH AS CABERNET SAUVIGNON OR MERLOT

12 FRESH FIGS, STEMMED AND HALVED, OR 8 DRIED MISSION FIGS, STEMMED AND FINELY CHOPPED

2 TABLESPOONS BALSAMIC GLAZE (PAGE 209)

2 TABLESPOONS FINELY CHOPPED FRESH PARSLEY FOR GARNISH

1. Preheat the oven to 325°F. Season the brisket liberally on all sides with salt and pepper. Choose a large, heavy roasting pan that will accommodate the brisket and vegetables. Place over medium-high heat and heat the oil. Brown the brisket for about 4 minutes per side, or until nicely browned. This will help give the sauce a deep brown color and rich flavor. Drain the fat.

2. Sprinkle the onions, carrots, squash, garlic, and thyme into the pan. Add the wine and figs and stir to combine with the vegetables.

Cover and bake for 3 to 3½ hours, or until the meat is fork-tender. Let cool. Place the meat and sauce in separate containers or lock-top plastic bags, cover if necessary, and refrigerate overnight.

3. The next day, place the meat on a carving board and cut against the grain into thin slices. Overlap the slices in an ovenproof high-sided serving dish.

4. Preheat the oven to 350°F. Remove the hardened fat from the sauce. Place the sauce in a saucepan over medium-high heat and cook for 3 to 5 minutes, or until slightly thickened. Add the balsamic glaze. Taste and adjust the seasonings. Pour over the meat.

5. Place in the oven and reheat for 30 minutes, or until the sauce is bubbling. Garnish with the parsley and serve immediately.

ADVANCE PREPARATION:
Make up to 3 days ahead through step 4, cover, and refrigerate. Remove any accumulated fat. Reheat in a 350°F oven for 30 minutes. Garnish just before serving.

THE CLEVER COOK COULD:
○ Purée the sauce with a hand blender for a creamier-style sauce.
○ Use leftover brisket to make a flavorful tomato-meat sauce for pasta or polenta.
○ Make brisket sandwiches using Horseradish Cream (page 134) as a condiment.

BLACK PEPPER STEAK

I make this steak dish, my husband's favorite, every fall to kick off the holiday season. Living in Paris years ago, we used to go from restaurant to restaurant looking for our favorite steak au poivre. This is my version based on all those bistros I visited, with a sauce that complements the juicy rib-eyes. Begin dinner with Two-Endive Salad with Pear, Walnuts, and Blue Cheese (page 79), and serve the steaks with Green Beans with Caramelized Red Onion and Mushroom Topping (page 180) and Potato Pancake Frittata (page 183). For dessert, consider Chocolate-Peppermint Pudding Cakes with Peppermint Stick Ice Cream (page 205).

RECOMMENDED WINE:

A subtly spicy red will pair seamlessly with this steak. Try a Chateauneuf du Pape or Syrah from France, an Australian Cabernet or Shiraz, or a California Cabernet or Merlot.

INGREDIENTS:

FOUR 1½-INCH-THICK RIB-EYE STEAKS

ONE 12-OUNCE JAR CRUSHED BLACK PEPPER

¼ CUP (½ STICK) UNSALTED BUTTER, OR MORE IF NEEDED

2 TABLESPOONS OLIVE OIL

4 SHALLOTS, FINELY CHOPPED

3 TABLESPOONS COGNAC

⅓ CUP RED WINE SUCH AS MERLOT OR CABERNET SAUVIGNON

1 CUP VEAL STOCK OR BEEF BROTH

⅓ CUP HEAVY CREAM

1 TEASPOON DIJON MUSTARD

SALT AND FRESHLY GROUND BLACK PEPPER

2 TABLESPOONS FINELY CHOPPED FRESH PARSLEY FOR GARNISH

1. Arrange the steaks in a single layer on a platter and then press the crushed black pepper evenly into both sides of the steaks, using your hands or the side of a cleaver. Let stand for 30 minutes.

2. In a large sauté pan or grill pan, melt the ¼ cup butter with the oil over medium-high heat until bubbling. Sear the steaks on one side and cook for about 4 minutes. Turn, sear the second side, and cook for 5 to 6 minutes, or until an instant-read thermometer inserted into the center of a steak reads 125°F for medium-rare. The steaks will continue to cook as they rest. Place on a platter and loosely cover with aluminum foil.

3. Add the shallots to the pan and sauté for 2 to 3 minutes, or until softened. You may need to add a bit more butter. Add the Cognac, raise the heat to high, and cook for 1 to 2 minutes, or until the alcohol evaporates. Add the red wine and boil for about 3 minutes, or until the sauce is slightly glazelike. Add the stock and cook for 5 minutes, or until the sauce is slightly thickened. Add the cream and mustard and whisk together. Cook for 1 minute, or until reduced slightly. Season with salt and pepper.

4. Cut the steaks into 2-inch slices and place a few pieces on each plate. Spoon the sauce over the steak slices, garnish with the parsley, and serve immediately.

THE CLEVER COOK COULD

- Serve the steaks family-style, sliced on a large platter.
- Make a green peppercorn sauce by omitting the black pepper crust and adding 2 tablespoons rinsed and drained green peppercorns to the sauce.
- Use leftover steak in a sandwich with horseradish cream (page 134).

STANDING RIB ROAST WITH HORSERADISH CREAM AND CABERNET SAUCE

❧ SERVES 8 ☙

When I was growing up, this was a standard dinner at my house. I loved to watch my father carve the juicy, rare slices and always hoped I would get the bone attached. Today this dish is a special-occasion treat because of its expense and its richness. In this recipe, a seasoning paste creates a crispy crust as well as extra flavor. I prefer horseradish cream with roast beef, but I also include a simple sauce for those who must have their gravy. Serve with Perfect Mashed Potatoes (page 185) and Braised Spinach with Crispy Shallots (page 175) for a memorable holiday dinner.

❧ **RECOMMENDED WINE:**
This classic holiday fare pairs beautifully with a soft-textured red such as a Cabernet Sauvignon or an aged Bordeaux. A perfectly mature red Burgundy or young Pinot Noir will be a match made in heaven. Don't be afraid to splurge!

INGREDIENTS:
HORSERADISH CREAM
⅓ CUP PREPARED CREAM-STYLE HORSERADISH

1 CUP SOUR CREAM

1 TEASPOON FRESH LEMON JUICE

SALT AND FRESHLY GROUND WHITE PEPPER

———

SEASONING PASTE
1 TABLESPOON SERIOUSLY SIMPLE SEASONING SALT (PAGE 208)

¼ TEASPOON FRESHLY GROUND BLACK PEPPER

1 TEASPOON DRY MUSTARD

2 TABLESPOONS ALL-PURPOSE FLOUR

1 TABLESPOON OLIVE OIL

———

ONE 3-RIB STANDING RIB ROAST, 6 TO 8 POUNDS, CHINE BONE REMOVED

1½ CUPS WATER

1 CUP CABERNET SAUVIGNON

1 CUP VEAL STOCK OR BEEF BROTH

SALT AND FRESHLY GROUND BLACK PEPPER

1. Make the horseradish cream: In a small bowl, stir together all of the ingredients until well blended. Taste and adjust the seasonings. Transfer to a serving bowl, cover, and refrigerate.

2. Preheat the oven to 450°F.

3. Make the seasoning paste: in a small bowl, stir together all of the ingredients until well blended.

4. Place a roasting rack in a large roasting pan. Set the rib roast on the rack fat-side up. Using your hands, carefully pat a thin coating of seasoning paste on the top and sides of the roast. Let stand for 30 minutes. Pour ½ cup of the water in the pan to help keep the pan from burning.

5. Place in the oven and roast for 20 minutes. Reduce the oven temperature to 350°F and roast for 1 to 1½ hours, or until an instant-read thermometer inserted in the center of the roast away from the bone reads 125°F for medium-rare. After 30 minutes, add another ½ cup water to keep the pan from burning and add the remaining ½ cup water after

another 30 minutes. Start checking for doneness after the roast has cooked for 1 hour to make sure you don't overcook it.

6. Transfer the roast to a carving board. Loosely cover with aluminum foil and let rest for at least 20 minutes. Remove the rack from the roasting pan.

7. Using pot holders, place the roasting pan on top of the stove. Skim off most of the fat and add the wine. Turn on the heat to medium-high and reduce the wine until it has thickened, scraping

up any brown bits. Add the stock and cook until the sauce is slightly thickened. Season with salt and pepper. Taste and adjust the seasonings. Pour into a gravy boat.

8. Carve the roast into thick or thin slices, as you prefer. Serve the horseradish cream and the cabernet sauce on the side.

ADVANCE PREPARATION:
Make the horseradish cream up to 4 hours ahead, cover, and refrigerate. Serve chilled. Make the seasoning paste up to 4 hours ahead, cover, and keep at room temperature.

BRAISED SHORT RIBS WITH GUAVA BARBECUE SAUCE

SERVES 6 TO 8

Try these meaty fork-tender ribs braised in an out-of-this-world barbecue sauce flavored with exotic guava nectar. This quintessential comfort-food dish has a surprising flavor that will have your friends and family begging for you to make the dish a holiday tradition. I like to serve the ribs with Potato Pancake Frittata (page 183) or Perfect Mashed Potatoes (page 185) and steamed broccolini.

RECOMMENDED WINE:
A supple, fruit-driven Zinfandel or a soft yet bright and refreshing white Zinfandel or blush wine will bring out the best in these braised short ribs.

INGREDIENTS:
5 POUNDS LEAN SHORT RIBS OF BEEF, PREFERABLY BONELESS, CUT INTO 3- TO 4-INCH PIECES

SALT AND FRESHLY GROUND BLACK PEPPER

3 TABLESPOONS CANOLA OIL

2 ONIONS, SLICED THICKLY INTO RINGS

4 CARROTS, PEELED AND CUT INTO ½-INCH SLICES

4 GARLIC CLOVES, FINELY CHOPPED

1 CUP FAVORITE BARBECUE SAUCE

1½ CUPS GUAVA NECTAR

2 TABLESPOONS FINELY CHOPPED FRESH PARSLEY FOR GARNISH

1. Preheat the oven to 450°F. Place the ribs in a large roasting pan and season them evenly on both sides with salt and pepper. Roast the ribs for 25 minutes. Turn them and roast for another 25 minutes, or until the ribs are very brown. Remove the ribs from the pan, blot with paper towels, and reserve. Reduce the oven temperature to 325°F.

2. Meanwhile, in a large nonstick Dutch oven or heavy flameproof casserole, heat the oil over medium-high heat. Cook the onions, stirring to prevent them from burning, for 10 to 12 minutes, or until brown and slightly caramelized. Add the carrots and sauté for 3 minutes, or until slightly softened. Add the garlic and sauté for 1 minute. Add the barbecue sauce and nectar, and bring to a boil over medium-high heat.

3. Place the ribs in the pot and spoon some of the vegetables over the ribs. Cover the pot and reduce the heat until the liquid is at a simmer. Transfer to the oven and braise for about 2½ hours, or until the meat is tender. Let come to room temperature and then cover and refrigerate. (It is best to do this overnight.)

4. Remove the top layer of fat from the sauce and any accumulated fat from the ribs. Gently reheat the ribs over medium heat and bring to a boil. Braise for about 10 minutes, or until the ribs are heated through and the sauce is simmering. Taste and adjust the seasonings. Place in a large serving bowl and garnish with the parsley. Serve immediately.

ADVANCE PREPARATION:
Make up to 3 days ahead, cover, and refrigerate. The ribs may also be frozen; defrost and gently reheat on top of the stove, adjusting the seasonings.

SERIOUSLY SIMPLE HOLIDAYS

136

GRILLED VEAL CHOPS WITH THYME AND BALSAMIC GLAZE

SERVES 4

Veal rib chops are a dish I reserve for special occasions, since they are quite expensive. I find that a simple marinade and a quick pan sauce work especially well for veal chops. The marinade, infused with balsamic vinegar and thyme, penetrates the tender meat, and the finishing sauce brings out its inherent qualities. I tend to serve this dish to a small group because of the last minute preparation required. Accompany with Green Beans with Caramelized Red Onion and Mushroom Topping (page 180) and Potato Pancake Frittata (page 183).

RECOMMENDED WINE:

Special occasions demand special wines. Uncork a reserve-style Chardonnay, perhaps one with a few years of bottle age, with extra complexity and richness to match the dish. Or a special silky Pinot Noir would work well.

INGREDIENTS:
MARINADE
¼ CUP OLIVE OIL

2 TABLESPOONS BALSAMIC VINEGAR

1 SHALLOT, FINELY CHOPPED

2 GARLIC CLOVES, MINCED

1 TABLESPOON CHOPPED FRESH THYME, OR 1 TEASPOON DRIED THYME

SERIOUSLY SIMPLE SEASONING SALT (PAGE 208)

FRESHLY GROUND BLACK PEPPER

———

FOUR 12-OUNCE VEAL RIB CHOPS

OLIVE OIL SPRAY

SALT AND FRESHLY GROUND BLACK PEPPER

———

GLAZE
1 CUP VEAL STOCK OR BEEF BROTH, OR ½ CUP VEAL DEMI-GLACE

1 TABLESPOON BALSAMIC GLAZE (PAGE 209)

2 TABLESPOONS CRÈME FRAÎCHE

SALT AND FRESHLY GROUND BLACK PEPPER

———

THYME SPRIGS FOR GARNISH

1. Make the marinade: In a small bowl, stir together all of the ingredients until blended. Taste and adjust the seasonings.

2. Place the veal chops in a lock-top plastic bag and pour in the marinade. Turn the chops in the bag to coat them evenly. Seal the bag and refrigerate for 2 to 4 hours.

continued on next page

. . . continued

3. Coat a large grill pan with olive oil spray. Heat the pan over high heat.

4. Season the veal chops with salt and pepper. Place in the hot pan and cook for 5 minutes. Turn and cook for 5 to 7 minutes on the second side. Quickly sear the edges all around, about 2 minutes. If the veal is still too raw, keep turning the chops every minute until the veal is very pink inside. Remove to a platter and cover with aluminum foil.

5. Make the glaze: In the grill pan over medium heat, combine the stock, balsamic glaze, and crème fraîche. Deglaze the pan by scraping up the brown bits. Season with salt and pepper and cook for about 2 minutes, or until the sauce has a glazelike consistency. Immediately pour over the veal chops.

6. Serve immediately, garnished with the thyme sprigs.

ADVANCE PREPARATION:
Make up to 4 hours ahead through step 1, cover, and refrigerate.

BRAISED LAMB WITH PARSNIPS AND CARROTS

SERVES 8 TO 10

My friend Laurie Burrows Grad shared this recipe with me. Perfect for a casual family dinner, the lamb slowly braises in the oven, allowing time with the family to do other things. This is a classic French recipe in which the lamb is cooked at such a low temperature over such a long time that it can almost be eaten with a spoon. Make sure to start a day ahead, since the lamb requires a night in the refrigerator before the sauce is finished. Serve with simple cooked noodles dressed with butter and parsley or with spaetzle.

RECOMMENDED WINE:

Comfort food like this lamb calls for comfort wine that is smooth and satisfying and won't bust the holiday budget. The richness of the lamb and sweetness of the vegetables will pair perfectly with an affordable Rhône-style red blended with Grenache, Syrah, and possibly some Carignan and Mourvèdre.

INGREDIENTS:

ONE 6- TO 8-POUND BONE-IN LEG OF LAMB

SERIOUSLY SIMPLE SEASONING SALT (PAGE 208)

FRESHLY GROUND BLACK PEPPER

2 TABLESPOONS OLIVE OIL

2 LARGE ONIONS, THINLY SLICED

2 CUPS DRY RED WINE

4 CUPS CHICKEN BROTH

ONE 14½-OUNCE CAN CRUSHED FIRE-ROASTED OR OTHER TOMATOES WITH JUICE

12 GARLIC CLOVES, PEELED

1½ TABLESPOONS CHOPPED FRESH THYME, OR 2 TEASPOONS DRIED THYME

6 CARROTS, PEELED AND CUT INTO 2-INCH SLICES

4 PARSNIPS, PEELED AND CUT INTO 2-INCH SLICES

2 TEASPOONS BALSAMIC GLAZE (PAGE 209)

2 TABLESPOONS CHOPPED FRESH PARSLEY FOR GARNISH

1. Preheat the oven to 275°F.

2. Make sure the lamb is totally trimmed of the "fell," the outer thin, papery covering. Trim away much of the fat as well. Season the lamb liberally with salt and pepper.

3. In a very large, deep Dutch oven or ovenproof casserole large enough to hold the lamb and liquid, heat 1 tablespoon of the oil over medium-high heat. Brown the lamb, turning it with tongs, for 5 to 8 minutes. Transfer the lamb to a platter. Drain off as much of the fat as you can from the pot and, using a slotted spoon, remove any dark brown or blackened bits.

Heat the remaining 1 tablespoon oil over medium heat and sauté the onions for 5 minutes, or until nicely softened. Add the wine, broth, tomatoes, garlic, and thyme to the pot and bring to a simmer. Add the carrots and parsnips.

4. Return the lamb to the pot, and arrange the vegetables around and on top of the lamb. Cover the pot and place in the oven. Braise the lamb for 6 to 7 hours, or until the meat is butter-tender and falling off the bone. Gently turn the meat after 3 hours. Let the lamb come to room temperature. Cover, and refrigerate overnight.

5. The next day, remove the hardened fat on the top. (I use disposable rubber gloves to do this.) Transfer the lamb to a platter. Bring the sauce to a simmer over medium-high heat. Add the balsamic glaze and reduce the sauce slightly, about 5 minutes. Season with salt and pepper. Taste and adjust the seasonings. Return the lamb to the pot and simmer for 5 minutes. Turn the lamb and finish reheating for about 5 minutes. Serve in the pot or arrange the lamb and vegetables on a large platter, ladling the sauce on top. Garnish with the parsley and serve immediately.

ADVANCE PREPARATION:
Make through step 4 up to 3 days ahead, cover, and refrigerate.

RACK OF LAMB WITH MUSTARD-DATE CRUST

SERVES 4 TO 6

This inventive preparation for rack of lamb is a holiday treat. Slightly sweet and mildly pungent, it is one of my favorite dishes to serve for an intimate party. Have your butcher remove the chine bone, trim the racks, and scrape the bones to make the lamb easy to prepare. For a pretty presentation, crisscross the ends of the lamb chops. Begin dinner with Mushroom and Potato Bisque with Pancetta Croutons (page 66) and serve the lamb with Roasted Brussels Sprouts (page 177).

RECOMMENDED WINE:
Serve with a deeply concentrated and flavored Syrah or a rich and robust Zinfandel.

INGREDIENTS:
MUSTARD-DATE PASTE
½ CUP COARSELY CHOPPED, PITTED DATES

⅓ CUP DIJON MUSTARD

1 TABLESPOON FRESH THYME LEAVES

2 TABLESPOONS OLIVE OIL

SALT AND FRESHLY GROUND BLACK PEPPER

———

TWO 2- TO 2½-POUND RACKS OF LAMB (8 CHOPS EACH), CHINE BONE REMOVED, TRIMMED OF EXCESS FAT, AND MEAT SCRAPED FROM EACH BONE 1½ INCHES FROM END

———

CRUMB COATING
¾ CUP PANKO OR OTHER DRIED COARSE BREAD CRUMBS

¼ CUP GROUND ALMONDS

2 SHALLOTS, FINELY CHOPPED

SALT AND FRESHLY GROUND BLACK PEPPER

3 TABLESPOONS OLIVE OIL

———

FRESH THYME AND PARSLEY LEAVES FOR GARNISH

1. Make the mustard-date paste: Combine all of the ingredients in a food processor fitted with the metal blade and process until puréed. Transfer to a small bowl.

2. Preheat the oven to 450°F. Place the racks of lamb bone-side down in a shallow roasting pan. Using a rubber spatula, smear one-fourth of the mustard-date paste on each of the racks to make a thin coating. Roast for 18 to 25 minutes for medium-rare. An instant-read thermometer inserted into the thickest part of the lamb should read 125°F for rare and 130°F for medium-rare.

3. Make the crumb coating: In a small bowl, stir together all of the ingredients until evenly blended.

4. Preheat the broiler. Using the rubber spatula, carefully spread the remaining mustard-date paste on each rack in an even layer, making sure not to remove the crust. Pat the crumb coating evenly on top. Place the lamb in the broiler about 6 inches from the heat and cook for 2 to 3 minutes, or until lightly browned. Do not let the crust burn.

5. To serve, place the racks on a platter or carving board and garnish with the thyme leaves. Cut between the bones to separate the chops. Serve 2 or 3 chops per person.

ADVANCE PREPARATION:
Make the mustard-date paste and crumb coating up to 4 hours ahead, cover, and keep at room temperature.

PINEAPPLE-HONEY-GLAZED HAM

❧ SERVES 12 TO 16 ☙

I had never been a ham lover—until I made this delectable sweet-and-savory ham. If your family enjoys ham for Christmas dinner, they will certainly like this recipe and be thrilled to have plenty of leftovers for the rest of the holiday. I also like to serve this dish on New Year's Day with assorted salads and condiments. Already cooked, spiral-sliced hams are now readily available at the supermarket. You'll find this variety especially convenient since it does not require carving. Accompany with Yam and Winter Squash Purée (page 178).

❧ **RECOMMENDED WINE:**
It's easy to complement the spice and sweetness of this ham dish with an off-dry Gewürztraminer. If your fondness is for red, celebrate with a fresh Beaujolais Nouveau.

INGREDIENTS:
GLAZE
ONE 8-OUNCE CAN CRUSHED PINEAPPLE

½ CUP ORANGE BLOSSOM HONEY

¼ CUP PACKED BROWN SUGAR

¼ CUP DIJON MUSTARD

¼ TEASPOON GROUND CLOVES

———

ONE 8-POUND COOKED SPIRAL-SLICED HAM

1. Preheat the oven to 325°F.

2. Make the glaze: in a small bowl, stir together all of the ingredients until well blended.

3. Place the ham flat-side down in a shallow roasting pan. Using bamboo skewers, skewer the ham in 2 places to hold the slices firmly together.

4. Bake for 1 hour. Spread half of the glaze on the ham, using the back of a spoon to help it adhere to the ham. Bake for 45 more minutes, or until an instant-read thermometer inserted into the center of the ham reads 135°F.

5. Raise the oven temperature to 425°F. Apply the remaining glaze, pressing it into the ham with the back of the spoon. Bake for 20 to 30 minutes, or until the glaze is set and the internal temperature of the ham is 140°F. Place on a carving board or platter. Remove the skewers and serve.

ADVANCE PREPARATION:
Make up to 1 hour ahead and serve warm. The ham can also be made 2 days ahead, refrigerated, and served chilled.

THE CLEVER COOK COULD:
○ Serve the ham chilled as a main-course luncheon along with chilled salads such as potato or pasta.
○ Make grilled ham and Gruyère sandwiches with honey Dijon mustard.
○ Add chopped ham to scrambled eggs or a frittata.
○ Use ham slices as a base for poached eggs.
○ Add chopped ham to your favorite macaroni and cheese.

ROAST LOIN OF PORK WITH MUSTARD CRUST

SERVES 6 TO 8

This recipe is so easy to make that it could well become a standard at your table during the holidays. Perfect for a large dinner party, this moist pork roast is complemented by a savory Cognac-mustard sauce and mustard applesauce. Serve with Braised Spinach with Crispy Shallots (page 175) and Rice Pilaf with Dried Cherries and Toasted Pistachios (page 189). Chocolate-Toffee Pie (page 201) would be a fitting finale.

RECOMMENDED WINE:

The two sauces are the keys, so match the sweet and spicy elements with a wine that delivers both. If white is your preference, select an off-dry Riesling. For a red, a supple yet spicy Shiraz or Zinfandel will be sublime.

INGREDIENTS:

MUSTARD APPLESAUCE

2 CUPS FAVORITE APPLESAUCE OR MAPLE-PEAR APPLESAUCE (PAGE 214)

2 TEASPOONS DIJON MUSTARD

MUSTARD COATING

½ CUP DIJON MUSTARD

2 TABLESPOONS MUSTARD SEEDS

1 TEASPOON DRIED THYME

1 TEASPOON SERIOUSLY SIMPLE SEASONING SALT (PAGE 208)

FRESHLY GROUND BLACK PEPPER

2 TABLESPOONS OLIVE OIL

ONE 3½-POUND PORK LOIN ROAST, TIED

COGNAC SAUCE

½ CUP COGNAC

1 CUP CHICKEN BROTH

3 TABLESPOONS CRÈME FRAÎCHE

1 TABLESPOON DIJON MUSTARD

PINCH COARSELY GROUND WHITE PEPPER

---

2 TABLESPOONS FINELY CHOPPED FRESH PARSLEY FOR GARNISH

1. Make the mustard applesauce: in a small serving bowl, stir together the applesauce and the mustard until blended. Cover and refrigerate until serving.

2. Make the mustard coating: in a small bowl, stir together all of the ingredients until well blended.

3. Preheat the oven to 375°F. Place the roast on a rack in a shallow roasting pan. Wearing disposable rubber gloves, spread the mustard coating evenly over the roast. Roast the pork for 1¼ to 1½ hours, or until an instant-read thermometer inserted into the center of the pork reads 140°F. Transfer the roast to a carving board, cover with aluminum foil, and let rest for at least 10 minutes. Place the roasting pan on the top of the stove.

4. While the roast is resting, make the Cognac sauce: Add the Cognac and broth to the roasting pan and turn on the heat to high. Bring to a boil and deglaze the pan

continued on next page

. . . continued

by scraping up the brown bits. Boil for about 3 minutes, or until the alcohol has evaporated and the liquid is slightly reduced. Whisk in the crème fraîche and mustard, bring to a boil, and cook for about 2 minutes, or until slightly thickened. Season with pepper and whisk well. Taste and adjust the seasonings. Just before serving, strain the sauce into a gravy boat or a serving bowl.

5. Remove the string from the loin and slice the pork. Arrange the slices on a platter and spoon some of the Cognac sauce on top. Garnish with parsley. Serve with the remaining Cognac sauce and the applesauce on the side.

ADVANCE PREPARATION:
Make the mustard applesauce and mustard coating 1 day ahead, cover, and refrigerate.

THE CLEVER COOK COULD:
- Make this dish using three 1¼-pound pork tenderloins and roasting them, without allowing them to touch, for 25 to 35 minutes. The sliced pieces will be smaller than the slices of loin.
- Apply the mustard coating to a leg of lamb before roasting.

SEAFOOD

SLOW-ROASTED SALMON WITH MISO VINAIGRETTE

When salmon is slowly roasted at a low temperature, the flesh acquires a creamy, moist texture. Here, a light Asian-style vinaigrette complements the salmon. Begin with Lime-Mint Slaw (page 83). Serve with a simple rice pilaf with peas and cilantro for a quick and satisfying dinner.

RECOMMENDED WINE:
Holidays are ideal for sparkling wines, and a refreshingly crisp brut will tame the saltiness and tang of the vinaigrette, as will a Sauvignon Blanc. Another option is a fruity, slightly sweet Riesling, a pleasing contrast to the vinaigrette.

INGREDIENTS:
VINAIGRETTE
2 TABLESPOONS WHITE MISO

1 TEASPOON PREPARED WASABI

2 TABLESPOONS RICE WINE VINEGAR

1 TABLESPOON OLIVE OIL

½ CUP FINELY CHOPPED ENGLISH CUCUMBER

————

2 POUNDS SALMON FILETS, CUT INTO 4 TO 6 EQUAL PIECES

1 TABLESPOON OLIVE OIL

SALT AND FRESHLY GROUND BLACK PEPPER

1. Make the vinaigrette: in a small bowl, whisk together all of the ingredients until well blended.

2. Preheat the oven to 275°F. Rub both sides of the salmon with the oil and season with salt and pepper.

3. Place the salmon skin-side down on a nonstick or aluminum foil–lined baking sheet. Roast for 18 to 20 minutes, or until flaky and just cooked through. The salmon will appear very moist.

4. Place the salmon on plates, drizzle with the vinaigrette, and serve immediately.

ADVANCE PREPARATION:
Make the vinaigrette up to 4 hours ahead, cover, and keep at room temperature.

ROASTED HALIBUT WITH PISTACHIO-PARMESAN CRUST

SERVES 4

In this simple, light dish, a delicious crust contrasts with the moist, meaty texture of the halibut. A few squirts of lemon bring all the flavors together. I roast the fish on a rack so the bottom and top cook evenly, and the crust stays intact. Serve with Pasta with Leeks and Peas (page 171) for an easy yet sophisticated dinner.

RECOMMENDED WINE:
For this simple dish, select a dry white wine with similar characteristics, such as an unoaked or lightly oaked Chardonnay, a lively Sauvignon Blanc, or Pinot Gris.

INGREDIENTS:

½ CUP UNSALTED RAW PISTACHIOS

½ CUP FRESHLY GRATED PARMESAN CHEESE

GRATED ZEST OF 1 LEMON

FRESHLY GROUND BLACK PEPPER

FOUR ½-POUND CENTER PIECES HALIBUT, ABOUT 1½ INCHES THICK

OLIVE OIL SPRAY

LEMON WEDGES FOR SERVING

1. In a mini food processor, grind the pistachios until very fine. Transfer them to a small bowl and add the cheese, lemon zest, and pepper to taste. Mix to combine.

2. Preheat the oven to 350°F. Place the halibut pieces on a sheet of waxed paper and coat generously on both sides with olive oil spray. Sprinkle the pistachio mixture on both sides of the fish and pat all over so that the coating adheres.

3. Place the fish on a rack in a shallow roasting pan. Roast for 15 to 20 minutes, or until flaky. Allow about 10 minutes for each inch of thickness. To crisp the top, turn on the broiler and broil the fish for 1 to 2 minutes. Serve immediately with the lemon wedges.

ADVANCE PREPARATION:
Make 4 hours in advance through step 2 (except for preheating the oven), cover loosely, and refrigerate.

THE CLEVER COOK COULD:
- Use sea bass instead of halibut.
- Serve the fish on a bed of arugula with cherry tomatoes and Parmesan cheese shards, tossed with a lemon vinaigrette.
- Apply the pistachio coating to chicken paillards or scallops before cooking.
- Substitute almonds for the pistachios.

GLAZED WHITEFISH WITH RED PEPPER AIOLI

SERVES 6

If you are looking for a quick holiday fish dish, this is the one.
The glaze is colorful with red peppers, tomato pesto, and green chives.
Serve with Braised Spinach with Crispy Shallots (page 175) and Roasted
Potato Wedges with Leeks and Thyme (page 184).

RECOMMENDED WINE:

The tangy mayonnaise needs a crisp, flavorful white to balance the tart lemon and piquant garlic. Try a fresh, aromatic Sauvignon Blanc, or seek out a young, vivacious nonoaked Viognier.

INGREDIENTS:

SIX 6- TO ½-POUND WHITEFISH FILLETS

½ CUP RED PEPPER AIOLI (PAGE 211)

1 TABLESPOON CHOPPED FRESH CHIVES FOR GARNISH

1. Preheat the oven to 450°F. Spray the broiler pan with oil. Place the fillets on the broiler pan and evenly spread enough aioli on top of the fillets to make a thin glaze. Roast for about 12 minutes, or until the flesh is opaque.

2. Preheat the broiler if necessary. Place the fillets in the broiler about 3 inches from the heat source and broil for about 2 minutes, or until the top browns. Do not let the fish burn. Sprinkle with the chives and serve immediately with the remaining aioli.

THE CLEVER COOK COULD:

- Use other firm fish like halibut or sea bass. You may need to roast the fish longer if it is thicker.
- Substitute 1 tablespoon chopped oil-packed sun-dried tomatoes for the sun-dried tomato pesto when making the Red Pepper Aioli.
- Add other herbs like parsley, basil, or thyme to the aioli.

PAN-SEARED SEA SCALLOPS WITH TOMATO-VODKA SAUCE

SERVES 6

I love this sophisticated recipe for a quick dinner for family or friends. The seared scallops with their creamy interiors are complemented by a tangy tomato sauce with just a touch of vodka flavor. Large sea scallops work best for this recipe because they will sear evenly and will not overcook as quickly as bay scallops. I like to accompany the scallops with Pasta with Leeks and Peas (page 171).

RECOMMENDED WINE:

The complexity of this dish demands a rich wine with layers of flavors. White or red can work equally well. Select a Sauvignon Blanc blended with Semillon and a touch of oak, or a Pinot Gris. For the red, try a light-bodied Pinot Noir.

INGREDIENTS:

SAUCE

1 TABLESPOON OLIVE OIL

1 LEEK, WHITE AND LIGHT GREEN PARTS ONLY, CLEANED AND FINELY CHOPPED

2 GARLIC CLOVES, MINCED

2 CUPS FAVORITE MARINARA SAUCE

2 TABLESPOONS SUN-DRIED TOMATO PESTO

3 TABLESPOONS VODKA

⅓ CUP HEAVY CREAM OR CRÈME FRAICHE

PINCH RED PEPPER FLAKES

SALT

½ CUP ALL-PURPOSE FLOUR

2 TEASPOONS SERIOUSLY SIMPLE SEASONING SALT (PAGE 208)

FRESHLY GROUND BLACK PEPPER

2 POUNDS LARGE SEA SCALLOPS, PATTED DRY

2 TABLESPOONS OLIVE OIL

3 TABLESPOONS VODKA

2 TABLESPOONS FINELY CHOPPED FRESH PARSLEY FOR GARNISH

1. Make the sauce: In a large skillet, heat the olive oil over medium heat. Sauté the leek for 3 to 5 minutes, until soft but not brown. Add the garlic and sauté for 1 minute. Add the marinara sauce, pesto, vodka, cream, red pepper flakes, and salt to taste. Bring to a simmer and cook for 3 to 5 minutes, or until the alcohol has evaporated. Taste and adjust the seasonings.

2. Combine the flour, the salt, and pepper to taste in a lock-top plastic bag. Place the scallops in the bag and seal. Shake the bag to dredge the scallops evenly.

continued on next page

. . . continued

3. In a large nonstick skillet, heat the oil over medium-high heat. When the oil is hot, cook the scallops in batches for 3 to 4 minutes per side, or until seared on the outside and just cooked and opaque in the center. Put all the scallops in the pan and reduce the heat to medium. Add the vodka and reduce the liquid to a glaze. Add half of the sauce and glaze the scallops, turning them to coat, 1 to 2 minutes.

4. Place the scallops on a platter or individual plates, top with the remaining sauce, garnish with parsley, and serve immediately.

ADVANCE PREPARATION:
Make the sauce up to 1 day ahead, cover, and refrigerate. Reheat gently, adjusting the seasonings.

THE CLEVER COOK COULD:
- Substitute 1 pound peeled and deveined medium shrimp for the scallops. Sauté the shrimp until pink, 2 to 3 minutes.
- Use basil pesto instead of sun-dried tomato pesto in the sauce.

HOLIDAY SEAFOOD GUMBO

SERVES 6 TO 8

My friend Ciji Ware tells me that while doing research in New Orleans for her novel *Midnight on Julia Street,* she learned that many Southerners make gumbo for the holidays. As the story goes, while you stir the roux, you think of all the family members and friends that you love and send them good wishes for the New Year. Microwaving the roux turns it the proper dark brown in a quarter of the time it needs to cook on top of the stove. The roux continues to cook as the vegetables soften and will become very dark. So think of your friends and family each time you stir the roux in the microwave.

This recipe is pretty easy to make if you have everything cut up and ready to go. You can enlist family or friends to help you and make the preparation a group activity. The dish includes the classic andouille sausage along with shrimp and lump crabmeat. You can use shrimp alone if crabmeat is too expensive, and you can omit the sausage if serving fish eaters only. The gumbo base should be made at least 1 day ahead, and preferably 2 days in advance, for the rich flavors to enhance each other. I like to serve the gumbo in bowls with a scoop of rice in the center. I also offer warm crusty bread to soak up the sauce.

continued on next page

. . . continued

RECOMMENDED WINE:

This festive, spicy dish demands a fruit-driven wine to stand up to the zesty seasonings. A white with a kiss of sweetness, such as a Riesling or Gewürztraminer, will deftly tame the heat. For a red, select a Gamay, Pinot Noir, or southern Rhône with light body and soft tannin that won't clash with the spices and seafood.

INGREDIENTS:

ROUX

½ CUP CANOLA OIL OR OTHER HIGH-HEAT COOKING OIL

½ CUP ALL-PURPOSE FLOUR

———

BASE

1 LARGE ONION, CHOPPED

1 RED BELL PEPPER, SEEDED AND DICED

1 GREEN BELL PEPPER, SEEDED AND DICED

2 CELERY STALKS, DICED

4 GARLIC CLOVES, MINCED

ONE 14½-OUNCE CAN DICED TOMATOES WITH JUICE

2 TABLESPOONS TOMATO PASTE

6 CUPS CHICKEN BROTH OR FISH STOCK

2 BAY LEAVES

2½ TO 3 TABLESPOONS CAJUN CREOLE SEASONING BLEND

SALT AND FRESHLY GROUND BLACK PEPPER

———

½ POUND ANDOUILLE SAUSAGE, CUT INTO 1-INCH SLICES

2 POUNDS LARGE SHRIMP (13 TO 15 PER POUND), PEELED AND DEVEINED

1 POUND LUMP CRABMEAT

1 TEASPOON FILÉ POWDER

2 TABLESPOONS FINELY CHOPPED FRESH PARSLEY FOR GARNISH

HOT PEPPER SAUCE FOR SERVING

1. Make the roux: In a 4-cup glass measuring cup, stir together the oil and flour until combined, making sure no lumps remain. Microwave on high for 2 minutes. Using pot holders to protect your hands, stir the roux with a wooden spoon. Repeat 3 times until the roux is dark brown or almost black (for a total of 8 minutes on high). You may need to microwave the roux for 1 minute longer. Again using pot holders, transfer the roux to a large pot.

2. Make the base: Place the pot over medium heat. Add the onion, bell peppers, and celery and sauté for 8 to 10 minutes, or until softened, scraping up any brown bits from the bottom of the pan. Add the garlic and sauté for 1 minute.

3. Add the tomatoes, tomato paste, broth, bay leaves, seasoning blend, and salt and pepper to taste. Bring to a boil over high heat, reduce the heat to a low simmer, and cook for about 20 minutes, or until slightly thickened.

4. Add the sausage, shrimp, and crabmeat and cook for 3 minutes, or until the sausage and shrimp are heated through. Add the filé powder and cook for 1 minute. Remove the bay leaves and discard. Taste and adjust the seasonings.

5. To serve, ladle into bowls. Garnish with the parsley and pass the hot sauce at the table.

ADVANCE PREPARATION:

Make up to 3 days ahead through step 3, cover, and refrigerate. Reheat gently until simmering.

CIOPPINO

SERVES 6 TO 8

Growing up in California, I had the opportunity to taste many different versions of this classic San Francisco seafood stew. Scoma's restaurant at Fisherman's Wharf still has its own fishing boat that comes in each day with fresh seafood. You might find swordfish instead of cod or sea bass, and more shrimp than crab, depending on the season. For one version of the stew, Lazy Man's Cioppino, the cracking and shelling are done for you. I prefer the ritual of opening the shellfish. Just make sure to set out plenty of napkins and empty bowls for the shells. Do ask your fishmonger to crack the crab for you, so diners can easily find the sweet meat. Feel free to tailor the seafood to what's on hand at your purveyor that day. What could be a better companion to this meal than a warm crusty loaf of sourdough bread? To begin, consider an antipasto platter (page 62). For dessert, try Dried Fruit Compote with Honey Mascarpone (page 192) and serve some biscotti on the side.

Sparkling wine or Champagne, especially a Blanc de Noir or rosé, will be the perfect complement to this festive dish. If you prefer a red, try a light-bodied Zinfandel, a fruity Merlot, or a Pinot Noir.

INGREDIENTS:
TOMATO BASE
¼ CUP OLIVE OIL

2 ONIONS, FINELY CHOPPED

1 CARROT, PEELED AND FINELY CHOPPED

4 GARLIC CLOVES, MINCED

ONE 26-OUNCE JAR FAVORITE MARINARA SAUCE

¼ CUP TOMATO PASTE

3 TABLESPOONS FRESH LEMON JUICE

2 CUPS FISH STOCK OR CLAM JUICE

2 CUPS DRY WHITE WINE SUCH AS SAUVIGNON BLANC

PINCH SUGAR

SALT AND FRESHLY GROUND BLACK PEPPER

———

4 TABLESPOONS OLIVE OIL

16 STEAMER CLAMS, WELL SCRUBBED

16 MUSSELS, WELL SCRUBBED

¼ CUP DRY WHITE WINE SUCH AS SAUVIGNON BLANC

1 POUND HALIBUT, SEA BASS, FLOUNDER, RED SNAPPER, LING COD, MONKFISH, OR SWORDFISH, CUT INTO 2-INCH CHUNKS

1 POUND SEA SCALLOPS

1 POUND LARGE SHRIMP (13 TO 15 PER POUND), PEELED AND DEVEINED

1 COOKED DUNGENESS CRAB, CRACKED AND CUT INTO PIECES

2 TABLESPOONS FINELY CHOPPED FRESH PARSLEY FOR GARNISH

1 LEMON, THINLY SLICED, FOR GARNISH

1. Make the tomato base: In a 6-quart nonaluminum Dutch oven or stockpot, heat the oil over medium heat. Sauté the onions and carrot for about 5 minutes, or until softened. Add the garlic and sauté for 1 minute. Add the marinara sauce, tomato paste, lemon juice, stock, wine, and sugar. Cook, partially covered, for 20 minutes, or until the alcohol has evaporated and the sauce has a nice flavor. Season with salt and pepper. Cover to keep hot.

2. In another large Dutch oven, heat 2 tablespoons of the oil over medium heat. Sauté the clams and mussels for about 2 minutes. Raise the heat to medium-high and add the wine. Cover and steam for about 3 minutes, or until the shells open. Transfer the shellfish and wine broth to the tomato base. Discard any clams or mussels that don't open.

3. Heat the remaining 2 tablespoons oil in the same pot over medium-high heat. Sear the fish, scallops, and shrimp, and sauté for about 3 minutes, or until just opaque. Add the crab and cook just until heated through. Transfer all of the seafood to the tomato base and mix to coat evenly. Cook over medium-high heat for about 3 minutes, or just until the stew simmers. Do not overcook the fish. Serve in deep bowls, garnished with the parsley and lemon slices.

ADVANCE PREPARATION:
Make up to 3 days ahead through step 1, cover, and refrigerate. Remove from the refrigerator 1 hour before cooking the seafood and gently reheat over medium heat until simmering.

CRACKED CRAB WITH LEMON-CHIVE MAYONNAISE

Chilly holidays and sweet, cracked crab go hand in hand. In California, much of the Dungeness crab harvest comes from the northern coast of California as well as Oregon and Washington, beginning around December 1. But for San Franciscans there is a rush of excitement when the local season opens in late November. I serve crab on Thanksgiving eve when I am tired of cooking. One of the simplest meals ever, it always garners rave reviews.

Find a good local source for crab that is brought in fresh daily and boiled, and ask the fishmonger to clean and crack if for you. Around the holidays you will need to place the order ahead to ensure you get part of the daily catch. You can make one or all three of the sauce recommendations. I like to serve vinaigrette and aioli in addition to the lemon-chive mayonnaise. For a complete dinner, accompany the crab with steamed artichokes or a green salad, along with crusty bread and a dry white wine. The mayonnaise makes an excellent dipping sauce for artichokes.

Fresh crab is a natural with a richly textured Chardonnay, but be careful not to choose one with too much oak. With the lemon-chive mayonnaise, a crisp, zesty Sauvignon Blanc comes to life. Don't forget that Champagne or sparkling wine goes with just about anything!

INGREDIENTS:
LEMON-CHIVE MAYONNAISE

1 CUP MAYONNAISE

2 TABLESPOONS FRESH LEMON JUICE

1 TABLESPOON FINELY CHOPPED CHIVES

SALT AND FRESHLY GROUND WHITE PEPPER

3 OR 4 DUNGENESS CRABS, 5 TO 6 POUNDS TOTAL, COOKED, CLEANED, AND CRACKED

RED PEPPER AIOLI (PAGE 211)

BASIC VINAIGRETTE (PAGE 210)

1. Make the lemon-chive mayonnaise: In a small bowl, whisk together all the ingredients until well blended. Taste and adjust the seasonings. Refrigerate in a tightly covered container until serving.

2. Arrange the crab on a platter. Provide a bowl for empty shells, crab crackers, and narrow crab forks for extracting every morsel of meat. Serve the mayonnaise, aioli, and vinaigrette on the side.

THE CLEVER COOK COULD:

- Use leftover crabmeat in a salad, cioppino, or a pasta sauce.
- Vary the condiments by adding chipotle chile powder to the Red Pepper Aioli, puréed roasted garlic to the lemon-chive mayonnaise, or your favorite herbs to the Basic Vinaigrette.

CHILLED WHITEFISH AND SALMON TERRINE WITH HERBED HORSERADISH CREAM

SERVES 6 AS A MAIN COURSE, 10 TO 12 AS A FIRST COURSE

Pretty, overlapping slices of this chilled terrine make an elegant main course for fish lovers. Accompany with mixed greens lightly dressed with Basic Vinaigrette (page 210). Make sure to have some sliced challah on the table to serve alongside. Since the terrine can be made a few days ahead, it is a convenient addition to other last-minute main courses on a buffet tale. This is a true crowd-pleaser at my holiday table for Rosh Hashanah and Hanukkah. Use prepared horseradish instead of the horseradish cream if you are keeping kosher.

INGREDIENTS:

¼ CUP OLIVE OIL

4 CARROTS, PEELED AND FINELY CHOPPED

3 LEEKS, WHITE AND LIGHT GREEN PARTS ONLY, CLEANED AND FINELY CHOPPED

OLIVE OIL SPRAY

4 LARGE EGGS

6 TABLESPOONS MATZO MEAL

1 CUP VEGETABLE OR CHICKEN BROTH

2½ TEASPOONS SALT

1 TEASPOON FRESHLY GROUND WHITE PEPPER

1 TEASPOON SUGAR

1½ POUNDS GROUND WHITEFISH OR A MIXTURE OF WHITEFISH, PIKE, AND BUFFALO FISH

¾ POUND SALMON FILLET, SKIN REMOVED, GROUND

JUICE OF 1 LIME

——————

HORSERADISH CREAM

½ CUP PREPARED HORSERADISH

¼ CUP OLIVE OIL

1 TABLESPOON WHITE BALSAMIC VINEGAR

2 TABLESPOONS CRÈME FRAÎCHE

JUICE OF ½ LIME

2 TABLESPOONS FINELY CHOPPED FRESH HERBS SUCH AS CHIVES, DILL, OR PARSLEY

——————

LEMON SLICES AND PARSLEY SPRIGS FOR GARNISH

1. In a medium skillet, heat the oil over medium heat. Sauté the carrots and leeks for 5 to 7 minutes, or until softened. Let cool for 10 minutes.

2. Preheat the oven to 350°F. Lightly coat a 9½-by-5½-by-2½-inch loaf pan with olive oil spray.

3. In a large bowl, beat the eggs and matzo meal with an electric mixer on medium speed until well combined. Add the broth, cooled carrots and leeks, salt, pepper, and sugar and beat until well blended. Add the whitefish and salmon and mix well, making sure the ground fish is completely blended with the other ingredients.

4. Pour the fish mixture into the prepared pan. Pick up the pan with both hands and slam down on the counter to remove any air bubbles. Sprinkle with the lime juice. Bake for about 50 minutes, or until a skewer inserted into the center comes out clean. Let cool for 30 minutes. Cover with aluminum foil and refrigerate overnight.

5. Make the horseradish cream: In a small bowl, whisk together all of the ingredients, making sure the oil

is emulsified. Taste and adjust the seasonings. Transfer to a serving dish, cover, and refrigerate.

6. To serve, run a knife around the edges of the pan and invert the terrine onto a sheet of aluminum foil. Invert it onto a rectangular platter. Cut into slices, overlapping them on the platter, and garnish with the lemon slices and parsley sprigs. Pass the sauce at the table.

ADVANCE PREPARATION:
Make the terrine and sauce 2 days ahead, cover, and refrigerate.

THE CLEVER COOK COULD:
- Serve the terrine on little matzo crackers and top with a dollop of horseradish cream as an appetizer.
- Arrange slices of the terrine and mixed greens on individual plates as a first course or brunch entrée.
- Add ¼ cup puréed cooked beets to the horseradish cream.

PASTA, VEGETABLES, AND SIDE DISHES

BAKED PASTA WITH TOMATO, RED PEPPER, AND SWEET ITALIAN SAUSAGE SAUCE

❧ SERVES 6 TO 8 ❧

During the holidays, baked pasta is a perfect dish for casual entertaining. In my first Seriously Simple book, I included a baked pasta that many of my readers tell me is reason enough to buy the book. I have modified that recipe, giving it a lighter sauce enriched with some cream. Arugula offers a pleasant, slightly bitter counterpoint to the red peppers and marinara sauce. Best of all, you can make the dish a day ahead and finish it in the oven just before serving. Offer a large mixed salad or Winter Chopped Salad (page 80) without the chicken to begin, and for dessert, try Dried Fruit Compote with Honey Mascarpone (page 192) or Apple Clafouti (page 200).

❧ RECOMMENDED WINE:

The complex sauce with its sweet, sour, salty, and bitter notes deserves a wine with enough character and adequate acidity to stand up to and balance these flavors but not too much fruit, alcohol, or oak to be overpowering or cloying. Italian red varietals such as Sangiovese or Barbera are great choices, as is lighter Zinfandel or Primitivo.

INGREDIENTS:
SAUCE
1 TABLESPOON OLIVE OIL

1 POUND SWEET ITALIAN SAUSAGE, CASINGS REMOVED

½ POUND CREMINI MUSHROOMS, SLICED

2 GARLIC CLOVES, MINCED

4 CUPS FAVORITE MARINARA SAUCE

ONE 12-OUNCE JAR ROASTED RED PEPPERS, RINSED, DRAINED, AND FINELY CHOPPED

1 CUP HEAVY CREAM

SALT AND FRESHLY GROUND BLACK PEPPER

―――――

SALT

1 POUND PENNE PASTA

1 CUP FRESHLY GRATED PARMESAN CHEESE

1 CUP FRESHLY GRATED ASIAGO CHEESE

ONE-HALF 6-OUNCE BAG ARUGULA LEAVES

1. Make the sauce: In a large, deep flameproof casserole, heat the oil over medium-high heat. Cook the sausage meat, breaking up the meat with a spoon, for about 5 minutes, or until no pinkness remains. Drain off most of the fat. Add the mushrooms and sauté for 4 minutes. Add the garlic and sauté for 1 minute. Add the marinara sauce and red peppers, reduce the heat to medium, and simmer for 5 minutes, or until the sauce begins to thicken. Add the cream, season with salt and pepper, and stir to combine. Cook for 3 to 5 minutes, or until the sauce begins to thicken. Taste and adjust the seasonings.

continued on next page

. . . continued

2. Preheat the oven to 375°F. Oil a 9-by-13-inch baking dish. Bring a large pot of water to a boil. Salt the water, add the pasta, and cook over high heat for 10 to 11 minutes, or until al dente. Drain well.

3. In a medium bowl, stir together the cheeses. Combine the pasta with the sauce in the pot. Add 1 cup of the blended cheeses and the arugula leaves, mixing well to combine. Spoon the mixture into the prepared dish and evenly sprinkle with the remaining blended cheeses.

4. Bake for about 30 minutes, or until the sauce begins to bubble and the cheese is browned. Serve immediately.

ADVANCE PREPARATION:
Make 1 day ahead through step 3, cover, and refrigerate. Remove from the refrigerator 2 hours before baking and uncover when baking.

THE CLEVER COOK COULD:
- Divide the pasta and sauce between 2 smaller baking dishes and freeze one before baking for up to 1 month.
- Add shredded cooked chicken or turkey instead of the sausage.
- Use the sauce as a filling for omelets or on top of polenta.
- Omit the sausage and use a total of 2 pounds cremini mushrooms, as well as 2 sliced zucchini, for a vegetarian version.

PASTA WITH LEEKS AND PEAS

Sometimes you just want a light side dish with your entrée. I like to serve this pasta, with its hint of olive oil and combination of sweet peas and leeks, when I want the entrée to stand out. It makes a delicious bed for Pan-Seared Sea Scallops with Tomato-Vodka Sauce (page 155). You could also serve it with a sprinkling of Parmesan as a light main course.

INGREDIENTS:

2 TABLESPOONS OLIVE OIL

2 LEEKS, WHITE AND LIGHT GREEN PARTS ONLY, CLEANED AND FINELY CHOPPED

½ POUND CREMINI MUSHROOMS, SLICED

2 GARLIC CLOVES, MINCED

1½ CUPS CHICKEN OR VEGETABLE BROTH

SALT

1 POUND DRIED OR FRESH PENNE OR FUSILLI

½ POUND FROZEN PETITS POIS, DEFROSTED

2 TABLESPOONS CAPERS, RINSED AND DRAINED

½ CUP JARRED ROASTED RED PEPPERS, RINSED, DRAINED, AND CHOPPED

FRESHLY GROUND BLACK PEPPER

2 TABLESPOONS FINELY CHOPPED FRESH PARSLEY

¼ CUP FRESHLY GRATED PARMESAN CHEESE (OPTIONAL)

1. In a deep skillet, heat the oil over medium heat. Sauté the leeks for 5 to 6 minutes, or until soft and lightly caramelized. Add the mushrooms and sauté for 4 minutes, or until softened. Add the garlic and sauté for 1 minute. Add the broth, cover, and cook for about 1 minute.

2. Bring a large pot of water to a boil. Salt the water, add the pasta, and cook according to the directions on the package. Drain and add to the skillet along with the peas. Cook over medium heat for 1 to 2 minutes, or until the peas are just tender. Add the capers, red peppers, salt and pepper to taste, and parsley and toss to combine. Taste and adjust the seasonings. Spoon into a serving dish and serve immediately. Offer the Parmesan on the side, if desired.

ADVANCE PREPARATION:
Make up to 4 hours ahead through step 1, cover, and keep at room temperature. Reheat before adding the pasta.

THE CLEVER COOK COULD:
- Omit the roasted red peppers and capers to make a variation that will go with many entrées.
- Add seeded and diced fresh red or yellow bell pepper instead of the roasted red peppers to the leeks and sauté for a few minutes to soften before adding the peas.
- Add sliced cooked chicken or turkey and serve as a main course.
- Add drained julienned sun-dried tomatoes packed in oil instead of the red peppers.

BUTTERNUT SQUASH LASAGNA

SERVES 10 TO 16

Using no-boil noodles and prepackaged peeled and cubed squash makes this dish a snap to put together. The creamy, sweet squash filling is enriched with mascarpone, and the simple white sauce is sparked with Dijon mustard. The lasagna makes an elegant first course, main course, or side dish on a buffet. You can also serve it to vegetarians at your Thanksgiving table. Start with Two-Endive Salad with Pear, Walnuts, and Blue Cheese (page 79).

RECOMMENDED WINE:

Light reds such as Pinot Noir, Sangiovese, or Chianti make fantastic partners as they beautifully cut through the richness of the cheese and the sweet squash. So will a crisp, barrel-aged Sauvignon Blanc. For the adventurous, a bottle of rosé bubbly will be a hit.

INGREDIENTS:

2 TABLESPOONS OLIVE OIL

TWO 1-POUND BAGS PEELED, SEEDED, AND CUBED BUTTERNUT SQUASH, OR ONE 3-POUND BUTTERNUT SQUASH, PEELED, SEEDED, AND CUT INTO 1½-INCH CUBES

SERIOUSLY SIMPLE SEASONING SALT (PAGE 208)

FRESHLY GROUND BLACK PEPPER

PINCH FRESHLY GROUND NUTMEG

¼ TEASPOON GROUND SAGE

1 CUP VEGETABLE OR CHICKEN BROTH OR WATER

½ CUP MASCARPONE CHEESE

———

WHITE SAUCE

6 TABLESPOONS UNSALTED BUTTER

6 TABLESPOONS ALL-PURPOSE FLOUR

4 CUPS MILK

2 TEASPOONS DIJON MUSTARD

SALT AND FRESHLY GROUND WHITE PEPPER

PINCH FRESHLY GROUND NUTMEG

———

1 POUND FRESH OR DRIED NO-BOIL LASAGNA NOODLES

2½ CUPS SHREDDED MOZZARELLA OR COMBINATION OF ITALIAN CHEESES, OR GRUYÈRE OR COMTÉ

1⅓ CUPS FRESHLY GRATED PARMESAN CHEESE

1. In a large skillet, heat the oil over medium-high heat. Add the squash, salt and pepper to taste, nutmeg, and sage and stir for about 2 minutes, or until evenly coated. Add the broth, cover, reduce the heat to medium, and cook for about 15 minutes, or until the squash is very soft. Uncover and, with the back of a large spoon or a potato masher, mash the squash. Add the mascarpone and mix to blend well.

2. Make the white sauce: In a medium saucepan, melt the butter over medium heat. Add the flour and whisk well until combined. Slowly pour in the milk and continue whisking until no lumps remain. Cook, whisking continually, for 5 to 7 minutes, or until the sauce coats a spoon. Add the mustard, salt and pepper to taste, and nutmeg and whisk to combine.

3. Oil a 9-by-13-inch baking dish. Preheat the oven to 375°F.

4. Spoon about ¾ cup of the white sauce evenly over the bottom of the dish. Top with a layer of noodles and then spread one-third of the squash mixture on top of the noodles. Sprinkle with ½ cup of the mozzarella and ⅓ cup of the Parmesan. Drizzle ½ cup of the white sauce over the cheese. Repeat the layers of noodles, squash mixture, cheeses, and white sauce 2 more times, and finish with a layer of noodles (for a total of 4 noodle layers). Spread the

remaining white sauce on top and then sprinkle evenly with the remaining 1 cup mozzarella and ⅓ cup Parmesan. Cover the dish tightly with aluminum foil and place on a baking sheet.

5. Bake the lasagna for 45 minutes. Turn on the broiler. Remove the foil and place the lasagna about 6 inches from the heat source. Broil for 2 minutes, or until the top is golden brown and the sauce is bubbling. Let rest for about 20 minutes and then cut into squares and serve immediately.

ADVANCE PREPARATION:
Make up to 2 days ahead through step 4, cover, and refrigerate. Remove from the refrigerator 1 hour before baking. The lasagna may be frozen after baking; defrost and reheat for about 20 minutes in a 350°F oven.

NOODLE KUGEL

❧ SERVES 8 TO 12 ❧

Children and adults all love this slightly sweet, comforting noodle pudding, a classic Jewish holiday dish. I use the crispy Japanese-style bread crumbs, called panko, for the topping because they add a crunchier texture than fine bread crumbs. Serve the kugel alongside Brisket with Figs and Butternut Squash (page 130) and Green Beans with Caramelized Red Onion and Mushroom Topping (page 180).

INGREDIENTS:

¾ POUND WIDE EGG NOODLES

4 LARGE EGGS

¾ CUP SUGAR

½ POUND CREAM CHEESE AT ROOM TEMPERATURE

1 CUP SOUR CREAM

¼ CUP (½ STICK) UNSALTED BUTTER, MELTED

2 CUPS COTTAGE CHEESE

1 TEASPOON VANILLA EXTRACT

2 GOLDEN DELICIOUS, GALA, OR PINK LADY APPLES, PEELED, CORED, AND FINELY CHOPPED

GRATED ZEST OF 1 ORANGE

TOPPING

1 CUP PANKO OR OTHER DRIED COARSE BREAD CRUMBS

⅓ CUP PACKED BROWN SUGAR

¼ TEASPOON GROUND CINNAMON

¼ CUP (½ STICK) UNSALTED BUTTER, MELTED

1. Preheat the oven to 350°F. Butter a 9-by-13-inch baking dish.

2. Bring a large pot of water to a boil and cook the noodles for about 6 minutes, or until al dente. Drain and set aside.

3. In a large bowl, beat the eggs with an electric mixer on medium speed or whisk until well blended. Beat in the sugar. Add the cream cheese, sour cream, butter, cottage cheese, and vanilla and whisk until the cream cheese is completely blended. Stir in the apples and orange zest and mix to blend. Stir in the drained noodles. Spoon into the prepared dish.

4. Make the topping: In a small bowl, combine the panko, brown sugar, cinnamon, and butter and mix with a fork to combine. Scatter the topping evenly over the noodles.

5. Bake for 1 hour, or until the kugel is set. Let rest for 15 minutes and then cut into squares and serve immediately.

ADVANCE PREPARATION:
Make up to 8 hours ahead through step 4, cover, and refrigerate. Remove from the refrigerator 1 hour before baking.

THE CLEVER COOK COULD:

○ Omit 1 apple and add ½ cup golden raisins.

○ Substitute 1 cup crushed pineapple for the apples, reducing the sugar to ⅔ cup.

○ Use low-fat sour cream, cottage cheese, and cream cheese for a lighter version.

BRAISED SPINACH WITH CRISPY SHALLOTS

SERVES 4 TO 6

This recipe is my standby for main dishes that require a light accompaniment with a green color. Try it with Plum-Glazed Turkey Breast with Sake and Pear Sauce (page 119) or Glazed Whitefish with Red Pepper Aioli (page 153).

INGREDIENTS:

3 TABLESPOONS OLIVE OIL

4 SHALLOTS, THINLY SLICED

3 GARLIC CLOVES, MINCED

SALT AND FRESHLY GROUND BLACK PEPPER

1 TABLESPOON UNSALTED BUTTER

1½ POUNDS BABY SPINACH LEAVES, CLEANED, OR TWO 12-OUNCE PACKAGES BABY SPINACH LEAVES

1 TEASPOON GRATED LEMON ZEST

1 TEASPOON FRESH LEMON JUICE

1. In a large Dutch oven, heat 2 tablespoons of the oil over medium-high heat. Sauté the shallots for 3 to 5 minutes, or until crisp and golden brown. Add the garlic and salt and pepper to taste, and sauté for 1 minute, making sure not to burn the garlic. Remove to a small bowl.

2. Add the remaining 1 tablespoon oil and the butter to the pot over medium heat. Add half of the spinach, pushing the leaves down into the pot and turning them with tongs. Cover tightly and steam for 2 to 3 minutes, turning the spinach with tongs after the first minute. Add the remaining spinach and turn with the tongs. Cover and cook for 2 minutes, or until the spinach just begins to wilt. Season with salt and pepper.

3. Uncover and cook the spinach, turning with tongs, for about 1 minute, or until wilted. The spinach should be bright green.

There will be excess liquid in the bottom of the pot; drain the spinach carefully, using a slotted spoon and pressing out the excess liquid. Sprinkle with the lemon zest and juice and toss to combine. Taste and adjust the seasonings.

4. Transfer to a platter or serving bowl. Top with the shallots and serve immediately.

ADVANCE PREPARATION:
Make up to 2 hours ahead through step 3, cover, and keep at room temperature. Reheat just before serving. Heat the shallots in a 350°F oven for 3 to 5 minutes.

THE CLEVER COOK COULD:
○ Drain the spinach well and add some sour cream or crème fraîche and Dijon mustard for a richer, creamy flavor. You can also purée it in the blender, leaving a bit of texture.

ROASTED BRUSSELS SPROUTS

❦ SERVES 4 TO 6 ❦

This is one of those dishes that you'll want to make again and again.
When roasted, the Brussels sprouts become caramelized, crispy green
nuggets with a creamy interior. The pomegranate seeds look like tiny red
jewels and offer a festive holiday touch. Serve these sprouts as a side dish
for simple grilled meats, roasted chicken, or roasted lamb. If you double
the recipe, use two baking sheets, place them on separate oven racks,
and switch them halfway through the roasting time.

INGREDIENTS:

2 POUNDS BRUSSELS SPROUTS,
TRIMMED AND HALVED IF LARGE

2 TABLESPOONS OLIVE OIL

SERIOUSLY SIMPLE SEASONING SALT
(PAGE 208)

FRESHLY GROUND BLACK PEPPER

2 TABLESPOONS POMEGRANATE
SEEDS FOR GARNISH

1. Preheat the oven to 425°F.
Arrange the Brussels sprouts on a
baking sheet. Drizzle with the oil
and sprinkle with salt and pepper
to taste. Using tongs, evenly coat
the sprouts with the seasonings.

2. Roast, turning the sprouts
once with the tongs, for about
25 minutes, or until golden
brown and cooked through.
The timing will depend on the
size of the sprouts.

3. Transfer to a serving bowl,
garnish with pomegranate seeds,
and serve immediately.

ADVANCE PREPARATION:
Make up to 4 hours ahead through
step 2. Cover and keep at room
temperature. Reheat in a 350°F
oven for about 10 minutes.

THE CLEVER COOK COULD:

○ Add ½ pound carrots, cut into
1-inch pieces, to the sprouts,
along with an extra tablespoon
of olive oil, and roast until the
carrots are tender.
○ Add Basic Vinaigrette (page 210)
to taste and serve as a salad.
○ Garnish with crumbled cooked
bacon and omit the pomegranate seeds.

YAM AND WINTER SQUASH PURÉE

❧ SERVES 6 ❧

If you and your family love yams and squash but don't like them too sweet, try this purée. Look for packages of peeled and cut-up vegetables for ease in preparation. If Japanese kabocha is available, use it in this recipe; it has a velvety texture. Serve the purée alongside any holiday meal. It goes well with Chicken Paillards with Cranberry-Port Sauce (page 106), Roast Turkey with Maple-Balsamic Butter Rub (page 112) and Make-Ahead Turkey Gravy (page 216), or Pineapple-Honey-Glazed Ham (page 144).

INGREDIENTS:

2 YAMS, PEELED AND CUT INTO 2-INCH CUBES, OR ONE 1-POUND BAG PEELED AND CUBED YAMS

ONE 1½-POUND WINTER SQUASH, PEELED AND CUT INTO 2-INCH CUBES, OR ONE 1-POUND BAG PEELED AND CUBED WINTER SQUASH

1 CUP CHICKEN OR VEGETABLE BROTH

3 TABLESPOONS MASCARPONE CHEESE

2 TABLESPOONS ORANGE MARMALADE

SERIOUSLY SIMPLE SEASONING SALT (PAGE 208)

FRESHLY GROUND WHITE PEPPER

2 TABLESPOONS FINELY CHOPPED FRESH PARSLEY FOR GARNISH

1. Combine the yams and squash in a large saucepan and pour in the broth. Cover and cook over medium-high heat for 12 to 15 minutes, or until the vegetables are soft enough to mash.

2. Mash the vegetables with a potato masher or put through a potato ricer and transfer to a bowl. Add the mascarpone and marmalade and mix with a spoon until well blended. Add salt and pepper to taste and blend. Taste and adjust the seasonings. Transfer to a serving bowl and garnish with the parsley. Serve immediately.

ADVANCE PREPARATION:
Make up to 1 day ahead, cover, and refrigerate. Bring to room temperature before reheating.

THE CLEVER COOK COULD:
- Garnish with a sprinkling of crushed ginger snaps or amaretti cookies for a textural contrast.
- Add pumpkin pie spice to the purée for a holiday flavor.

PARSNIP AND TURNIP PURÉE

⟅ SERVES 6 TO 8 ⟆

Try this tasty tribute to those unappreciated root vegetables for a
holiday side dish. Your guests will wonder how anything this rich tasting
can still be good for you. The vegetables turn a beige color, so be sure
to garnish with parsley. I like to serve the purée with Turkey with Orange-
Herb Basting Sauce (page 121) or as a bed for Roasted Halibut with
Pistachio-Parmesan Crust (page 152).

INGREDIENTS:

2 TABLESPOONS UNSALTED BUTTER

2 TABLESPOONS OLIVE OIL

1 ONION, FINELY CHOPPED

1 POUND WHITE TURNIPS, PEELED
AND CUT INTO 1-INCH CUBES

2 POUNDS PARSNIPS, PEELED AND
CUT INTO 1-INCH CUBES

2 GARLIC CLOVES, MINCED

2 CUPS VEGETABLE OR CHICKEN
BROTH

SALT AND FRESHLY GROUND WHITE
PEPPER

2 TABLESPOONS HEAVY CREAM
(OPTIONAL)

2 TABLESPOONS FINELY CHOPPED
FRESH PARSLEY FOR GARNISH

1. In a large skillet or shallow
flameproof casserole, melt the
butter with the oil over medium-
high heat. Sauté the onion for 3 to
5 minutes, or until softened. Add
the turnips and parsnips and sauté,
stirring to coat them, for about
3 minutes. Add the garlic and sauté
for 1 minute. Add the broth, bring
to a simmer, cover, and cook for
15 to 17 minutes, or until the
vegetables are tender.

2. In a food processor fitted
with the metal blade, process the
vegetables until smooth. Add salt
and pepper to taste and the cream
(if desired) and process to purée.
Taste and adjust the seasonings.

3. To serve, transfer the purée to a
serving bowl and garnish with the
parsley. Serve immediately.

ADVANCE PREPARATION:
Make up to 1 day ahead, cover,
and refrigerate. Gently reheat in a
saucepan just before serving.

THE CLEVER COOK COULD:
- Serve the purée as a bed for
  seared fish or chicken.
- Spoon into a shallow casserole,
  dot with bread crumbs and
  butter, and bake until the top
  is brown and crispy.

GREEN BEANS WITH CARAMELIZED RED ONION AND MUSHROOM TOPPING

SERVE 8 TO 10

Green beans seem to be a family favorite. I like to serve this simple yet flavorful side dish instead of the creamy green bean classic. It is perfect for Thanksgiving dinner since it can be doubled easily and transports well.

INGREDIENTS:

2 TABLESPOONS OLIVE OIL

½ POUND CREMINI MUSHROOMS, COARSELY CHOPPED

2 TABLESPOONS UNSALTED BUTTER

1 RED ONION, FINELY CHOPPED

1 TEASPOON BALSAMIC VINEGAR

1 GARLIC CLOVE, MINCED

2 TABLESPOONS FINELY CHOPPED FRESH PARSLEY

SALT AND FRESHLY GROUND BLACK PEPPER

2 POUNDS TENDER GREEN BEANS, ENDS REMOVED

1. In a medium skillet, heat 1 tablespoon of the oil over medium heat. Sauté the mushrooms for 3 to 4 minutes, or until they change color and soften. Remove to a bowl.

2. Add the remaining 1 tablespoon oil and 1 tablespoon of the butter. Sauté the onion for 7 to 10 minutes, or until it is soft and begins to caramelize. Add the vinegar and cook, stirring constantly, for 1 minute. Add the garlic and sauté for 1 minute. Add the mushrooms, parsley, and salt and pepper to taste. Remove from the heat.

3. Bring a large saucepan of water to a boil. Salt the water, immerse the beans in the boiling water, and cook for 5 to 7 minutes, or until tender but slightly resistant. Drain and place in a serving dish. Toss with the remaining 1 tablespoon butter and salt and pepper to taste. Sprinkle evenly with the topping and serve immediately.

ADVANCE PREPARATION:
Make 1 day ahead through step 1, cover, and refrigerate. Reheat the topping in a skillet before serving.

POLENTA WITH BUTTERNUT SQUASH AND CHESTNUTS

꩜ SERVES 6 TO 8 ꩜

I love this comforting dish. You can serve it as a vegetarian entrée or as a side for Chicken Paillards with Cranberry-Port Sauce (page 106), Rack of Lamb with Mustard-Date Crust (page 143), or Roast Duck Legs with Caramelized Shallots and Garlic (page 127).

INGREDIENTS:

2 TABLESPOONS OLIVE OIL

1 RED ONION, HALVED AND THINLY SLICED

SALT AND FRESHLY GROUND BLACK PEPPER

ONE 1½-POUND BUTTERNUT SQUASH, PEELED, SEEDED, AND CUT INTO 1-INCH CUBES, OR ONE 1-POUND BAG PEELED, SEEDED, AND CUBED BUTTERNUT SQUASH

2 GARLIC CLOVES, MINCED

1 TEASPOON FRESH THYME LEAVES, OR ½ TEASPOON DRIED THYME

1 CUP VACUUM-PACKED COOKED CHESTNUTS, HALVED

¾ CUP CHICKEN OR VEGETABLE BROTH

1 TABLESPOON BALSAMIC GLAZE (PAGE 209)

2 TABLESPOONS FINELY CHOPPED FRESH PARSLEY

―――――

POLENTA

7 CUPS CHICKEN OR VEGETABLE BROTH

½ TEASPOON SALT

1 CUP FRESH OR FROZEN CORN KERNELS

2 CUPS INSTANT POLENTA

1. In a large skillet, heat the oil over medium-high heat. Sauté the onion for 7 to 10 minutes, or until nicely caramelized. Season with salt and pepper.

2. Add the squash and sauté for 3 to 5 minutes, or until evenly coated. Add the garlic and thyme and sauté for 1 minute. Add the chestnuts and broth, cover, and cook for 5 to 7 minutes, or until the squash is fork-tender. Remove from the heat and add the balsamic glaze. Return to the heat and cook for 2 to 3 minutes, or until nicely glazed. Stir in the parsley. Taste and adjust the seasonings. Cook for a few minutes longer if any excess moisture remains.

3. Make the polenta: In a large, deep saucepan, bring the broth and salt to a rolling boil. Add the corn. Very slowly add the polenta in a thin stream, stirring constantly with a wooden spoon. Reduce the heat to low and cook, stirring constantly so the polenta doesn't stick, for 3 to 5 minutes, or until very smooth and stiff. Add the squash mixture and stir well to blend. Spoon into a serving bowl and serve immediately.

ADVANCE PREPARATION:
Make up to 4 hours ahead through step 2, cover, and keep at room temperature.

═══════════════

THE CLEVER COOK COULD:
- Omit the polenta for a simple side dish.
- Stir a few tablespoons of mascarpone cheese into the polenta for extra richness just before adding the squash mixture.

═══════════════

POTATO PANCAKE FRITTATA

❧ SERVES 4 ❧

This is an easy alternative to making individual potato pancakes.
It looks like a round, flat pancake and cooks similarly to a frittata, hence its
name. Amazingly enough, you need only one potato to prepare a 9-inch
pancake. I like to serve the frittata with Brisket with Figs and Butternut
Squash (page 130). Don't forget the Maple-Pear Applesauce
(page 214) and sour cream.

INGREDIENTS:

½ ONION, QUARTERED

1 LARGE EGG

2 TABLESPOONS FRESH PARSLEY
LEAVES

1 RUSSET POTATO, PEELED AND CUT
INTO 2-INCH CHUNKS

SALT AND FRESHLY GROUND BLACK
PEPPER

1 TABLESPOON MATZO MEAL OR PLAIN
BREAD CRUMBS

¼ TEASPOON BAKING POWDER

PEANUT, CANOLA, OR CORN OIL

1. Preheat the oven to 425°F.

2. In a food processor fitted with the metal blade, purée the onion and egg until smooth and fluffy. Add the parsley and potato and pulse until the mixture is finely chopped but still retains some texture. Season with salt and pepper, add the matzo meal and baking powder, and quickly process to combine. Do not overprocess. Pour the batter into a medium bowl.

3. Pour the oil about ⅛ inch deep into a 9-inch nonstick skillet with an ovenproof handle (or cover a wooden handle with aluminum foil) or into a cast-iron skillet. Heat over medium-high heat until the oil is hot (it will shimmer). Pour the batter into the pan and smooth the top. Cook, shaking the pan occasionally and moving the bottom of the batter with a wide spatula. Adjust the heat to make sure the bottom doesn't burn. Cook for at least 5 minutes, or until the bottom is nicely browned.

4. Transfer the skillet to the oven and bake the frittata for 10 to 15 minutes, or until slightly puffed and light brown. Carefully invert onto a 12-inch round platter, placing a spatula underneath the frittata to help it slide out easily.

Make sure that the browned top faces up. (You can also serve the frittata right out of the skillet.) Cut into wedges and serve immediately.

THE CLEVER COOK COULD:

- Double the recipe and use 2 nonstick skillets.
- Make Crispy Potato Pancakes with Sour Cream: Double the recipe. For each 4-inch pancake, place 3 to 4 tablespoons batter in a large nonstick skillet with 1 inch of vegetable oil on medium-high heat. Yield will be 12 to 14 pancakes. You can multiply the recipe further to make a large quantity.
- Serve as an appetizer garnished with sour cream, sliced smoked salmon, and caviar.
- Serve as a side dish to scrambled eggs or an accompaniment to simple grilled or roasted entrées.

ROASTED POTATO WEDGES WITH LEEKS AND THYME

❦ SERVES 6 TO 8 ❦

You'll appreciate these crispy potato wedges for their versatility in menu planning. Serve them with Scrambled Eggs with Caramelized Onions, Smoked Salmon, and Herbed Cream Cheese (page 97). They also are a perfect accompaniment to Black Pepper Steak (page 132) or Standing Rib Roast with Horseradish Cream and Cabernet Sauce (page 134).

INGREDIENTS:

2½ POUNDS RUSSET, YELLOW FINN, OR YUKON GOLD POTATOES, UNPEELED, RINSED AND PATTED DRY

3 TABLESPOONS OLIVE OIL

1 LEEK, WHITE AND LIGHT GREEN PARTS ONLY, CLEANED AND FINELY CHOPPED

1 TEASPOON FRESH THYME LEAVES, OR ½ TEASPOON DRIED THYME

1 TEASPOON SERIOUSLY SIMPLE SEASONING SALT (PAGE 208)

FRESHLY GROUND BLACK PEPPER

2 TABLESPOONS FINELY CHOPPED FRESH PARSLEY FOR GARNISH

1. Preheat the oven to 425°F. Oil a nonstick baking sheet.

2. Cut each potato in half and then cut into 2-inch wedges. In a large bowl, combine the oil, leek, thyme, salt, and pepper to taste and mix well. Add the potato wedges and toss until evenly coated.

3. Arrange the potato wedges in one layer on the prepared sheet. Roast for about 35 minutes, turning the wedges about every 10 minutes to prevent them from sticking to the pan. The potatoes are done when tender and golden brown.

4. Transfer the potatoes to a large serving dish and toss with the parsley. Serve immediately.

ADVANCE PREPARATION:
Make up to 2 hours ahead through step 3 and keep at room temperature. Reheat in a 350°F oven for 10 to 15 minutes and then toss with the parsley just before serving.

PERFECT MASHED POTATOES

SERVES 8 TO 10

Using Yukon Gold potatoes gives this side dish a rich, creamy texture that is hard to match with other potato varieties. The addition of both unsalted butter and a good-quality extra-virgin olive oil makes the mashed potatoes especially velvety. I like the skins in my mashed potatoes, but if you don't, peel the potatoes. Serve the mashed potatoes with Braised Short Ribs with Guava Barbecue Sauce (page 136) or Roast Turkey with Maple-Balsamic Butter Rub (page 112).

INGREDIENTS:

4 POUNDS YUKON GOLD OR OTHER YELLOW-FLESHED POTATOES, OR RED OR WHITE POTATOES, CUT INTO 3-INCH PIECES

8 GARLIC CLOVES, PEELED AND HALVED LENGTHWISE

1 TEASPOON SALT

3 TABLESPOONS UNSALTED BUTTER

2 TABLESPOONS EXTRA-VIRGIN OLIVE OIL

1¼ CUPS MILK OR HALF-AND-HALF

SALT AND FRESHLY GROUND WHITE PEPPER

1. Bring a large pot of water to a boil. Add the potatoes, garlic, and salt and simmer, partially covered, over medium heat for 15 to 20 minutes, or until the potatoes and garlic are fork-tender.

2. Drain the potatoes and garlic and return to the pot over high heat. Cook, tossing the potatoes, for 1 to 2 minutes, or until all the moisture is evaporated. Transfer to a large bowl and mash with a potato masher.

3. In a medium saucepan, heat the butter, oil, and milk over medium heat until the butter has melted. Add to the potatoes and whip with a wooden spoon or whisk to a smooth but not soupy consistency. Mash any pieces of garlic until totally puréed. When the liquid is absorbed, season with salt and pepper to taste. Transfer to a serving bowl and serve immediately.

ADVANCE PREPARATION:
Make up to 4 hours ahead, cover, and keep at room temperature. Reheat gently in the top of a double boiler over medium heat, adding extra milk as needed and adjusting the seasonings.

THE CLEVER COOK COULD:
- Peel the potatoes and purée with a potato ricer for a very smooth consistency.
- Add ⅓ cup freshly grated Parmesan cheese or 1 or 2 tablespoons prepared horseradish or a squirt of wasabi paste.
- Add 3 finely chopped leeks sautéed in olive oil to the mashed potatoes just before serving.

PASTA, VEGETABLES, AND SIDE DISHES

185

CORNBREAD, OYSTER, AND RED PEPPER STUFFING

SERVES 8 TO 10

Oysters and cornbread partner beautifully in this memorable stuffing that goes well with turkey, chicken, or duck. Pick up your favorite prepared cornbread, making sure it is not too sweet. This recipe makes enough to stuff a 16-pound bird, with leftovers to fill a medium casserole.

INGREDIENTS:

8 CUPS CUBED (1½-INCH) CORNBREAD

5 TABLESPOONS UNSALTED BUTTER

4 TABLESPOONS OLIVE OIL

3 LEEKS, LIGHT GREEN AND WHITE PARTS ONLY, CLEANED AND FINELY CHOPPED

5 CELERY STALKS, SLICED

1 RED BELL PEPPER, SEEDED AND CUT INTO ½-INCH PIECES

2 GARLIC CLOVES, MINCED

TWO 10-OUNCE JARS OYSTERS, DRAINED

½ CUP FINELY CHOPPED FRESH PARSLEY

SALT AND FRESHLY GROUND BLACK PEPPER

1 TEASPOON FINELY CHOPPED FRESH SAGE, OR ½ TEASPOON DRIED SAGE

1 TEASPOON FINELY CHOPPED FRESH THYME, OR ½ TEASPOON DRIED THYME

2 LARGE EGGS, WELL BEATEN

½ CUP CHICKEN OR TURKEY BROTH

1. Preheat the oven to 325°F. Place the cornbread on a baking sheet. Toast for 30 minutes, or until lightly browned; turn after 15 minutes to brown evenly. Or place the bread on a baking sheet and let sit out overnight, turning at least once, until dried out.

2. In a large skillet, melt 3 tablespoons of the butter with 2 tablespoons of the oil over medium heat. Sauté the leeks for 5 to 7 minutes, or until softened and lightly caramelized. Add the remaining 2 tablespoons butter and 2 tablespoons oil and sauté the celery and red bell pepper for 3 to 5 minutes, or until slightly softened. Add the garlic and sauté for 1 minute. Transfer to a large bowl.

3. Add the toasted cornbread, oysters, parsley, salt and pepper to taste, sage, and thyme and mix well. Taste and adjust the seasonings. Slowly add the eggs and broth, mixing carefully and making sure that the stuffing is moist but not too compact, especially if you are planning to stuff a turkey.

4. Stuff the turkey (see page 113) or oil a 2-quart baking dish and add the stuffing. The stuffing can be compacted because it will not expand in the pan. Cover tightly with aluminum foil.

5. Preheat the oven to 375°F. Bake the stuffing for 30 minutes. Remove the foil and bake for 15 more minutes, or until the top is brown. Serve immediately.

ADVANCE PREPARATION:
Make up to 1 day ahead through step 3, cover, and refrigerate. Remove from the refrigerator 1 hour before baking.

SAUSAGE, DRIED FRUIT, AND NUT STUFFING

❧ SERVES 8 TO 12 ❧

My friend Kathy Blue, the queen of Thanksgiving and co-author of *Thanksgiving Dinner*, suggested I use trail mix to make this delicious stuffing. You can serve it in a large casserole or stuff it into a 16-pound turkey with some left over to bake separately in a medium casserole. Either way, the crispy, nutty fruit flavors are a holiday hit. Make sure to start this a day ahead to dry out the bread.

INGREDIENTS:

1-POUND LOAF CIABATTA OR FRENCH BREAD, CUT INTO 1½-INCH CUBES (ABOUT 8 CUPS)

3 TABLESPOONS UNSALTED BUTTER

3 TABLESPOONS OLIVE OIL

2 ONIONS, FINELY CHOPPED

6 CELERY STALKS, COARSELY CHOPPED

SALT AND FRESHLY GROUND BLACK PEPPER

1 POUND UNCOOKED CHICKEN-APPLE SAUSAGE, CASINGS REMOVED

1 CUP VACUUM-PACKED COOKED CHESTNUTS, COARSELY CHOPPED

1½ CUPS NUT AND DRIED FRUIT TRAIL MIX, COARSELY CHOPPED

1 TABLESPOON FINELY CHOPPED FRESH THYME, OR 1 TEASPOON DRIED THYME

1 TABLESPOON FINELY CHOPPED FRESH SAGE, OR 1 TEASPOON DRIED SAGE

½ CUP FINELY CHOPPED FRESH PARSLEY

1¼ CUPS CHICKEN BROTH OR EASY TURKEY STOCK (PAGE 217)

3 TABLESPOONS UNSALTED BUTTER, CUT INTO SMALL PIECES

1. Preheat the oven to 325°F. Place the bread on a baking sheet. Toast for 30 minutes, or until lightly browned; turn after 15 minutes to brown evenly. Or place the bread on a baking sheet and let sit out overnight, turning at least once, until dried out.

2. In a large skillet, melt the butter with the oil over medium heat. Sauté the onions for about 5 minutes, or until softened. Add the celery and sauté for about 4 minutes, or until crisp-tender. Season with salt and pepper. Transfer to a large bowl.

3. In the same pan, brown the sausage for about 5 minutes, stirring occasionally to break up the meat and to keep it from burning. Let cool and add to the vegetables. Add the chestnuts, trail mix, thyme, sage, parsley, and bread cubes. Mix to combine. Season with salt and pepper. Slowly add the broth, mixing carefully and making sure that the stuffing is moist but not too com-pact, especially if you are planning to stuff a turkey. Taste and adjust the seasonings.

4. Stuff the turkey (see page 113) or oil a 2-quart baking dish and add the stuffing. Dot the top with the butter. The stuffing can be compacted because it will not expand in the pan. Cover tightly with aluminum foil.

5. Preheat the oven to 375°F. Bake the stuffing for 30 minutes. Remove the foil and bake 15 more minutes, or until the top is brown. Serve immediately.

ADVANCE PREPARATION:
Make up to 2 days ahead through step 3, cover, and refrigerate. Remove from the refrigerator 1 hour before baking.

THE CLEVER COOK COULD:
- Use precooked chicken-apple sausage and coarsely chop after browning.

RICE PILAF WITH DRIED CHERRIES AND TOASTED PISTACHIOS

This is a perfect side dish for poultry dishes, such as Roast Duck Legs with Caramelized Shallots and Garlic (page 127) or Cornish Hens with Braised Cabbage and Apple (page 110).

INGREDIENTS:

¼ CUP UNSALTED RAW PISTACHIOS

2 TABLESPOONS OLIVE OIL

3 SCALLIONS, WHITE AND LIGHT GREEN PARTS ONLY, THINLY SLICED

1½ CUPS LONG-GRAIN RICE

¼ CUP UNSWEETENED DRIED PITTED CHERRIES

3 CUPS HOT WATER OR VEGETABLE OR CHICKEN BROTH

SALT AND FRESHLY GROUND BLACK PEPPER

2 TABLESPOONS FINELY CHOPPED FRESH PARSLEY

1. Heat a small skillet over medium-low heat. Add the pistachios and toss gently for 2 to 3 minutes, or until they begin to brown lightly. Remove to a small bowl.

2. In a medium saucepan, heat the oil over medium heat. Sauté the scallions for 2 minutes, or until softened.

3. Raise the heat to high. Sauté the rice for about 3 minutes, or until well coated and lightly browned. Add the cherries and stir to combine. Reduce the heat to medium, add the hot water, stir with a fork, and bring to a boil. Cover and reduce the heat to low.

4. Simmer for about 20 minutes, or until all liquid has been absorbed and the rice is tender. Season with salt and pepper and add the parsley and pistachios. Taste and adjust the seasonings. Serve immediately.

ADVANCE PREPARATION:
Make 2 hours ahead and keep at room temperature. Reheat carefully in the top of a double boiler over medium heat for 10 minutes.

THE CLEVER COOK COULD:
○ Make a vegetable pilaf: Add 1 finely diced carrot when sautéing the rice and 1 cup defrosted frozen petits pois or 2 cups baby spinach leaves after the rice is tender and cook for about 3 minutes.
○ Add dried cranberries or apricots instead of the cherries, and almonds or pine nuts instead of the pistachios.

DESSERTS

DRIED FRUIT COMPOTE WITH HONEY MASCARPONE

✳ SERVES 6 TO 8 ✳

The honey and mascarpone topping is the perfect counterpoint to the slightly sweet-tart poached fruit. This is a wonderful finish for a Jewish holiday meal because it symbolizes the sweetness of the New Year. I like to accompany the compote with a plate of biscotti.

INGREDIENTS:

¾ POUND DRIED WHOLE PITTED APRICOTS

¾ POUND DRIED WHOLE PITTED PLUMS

½ POUND DRIED PITTED CHERRIES

3 ASIAN PEARS, PEELED, CORED, AND FINELY CHOPPED

⅓ CUP SUGAR

3 CUPS JOHANNISBURG RIESLING

2 CUPS WATER

TOPPING

ONE 5-OUNCE TUB MASCARPONE CHEESE

½ CUP HEAVY CREAM

2 TABLESPOONS HONEY

1. In a large, heavy saucepan, mix together the dried fruits, pears, sugar, wine, and water. Bring to a boil over medium-high heat. Reduce the heat to low and simmer, partially covered and stirring occasionally, for 20 to 25 minutes, or until the dried fruits are softened, the pears are slightly al dente, and the liquid is thickened.

2. Meanwhile, make the topping: In a medium bowl, combine the mascarpone, heavy cream, and honey. With an electric mixer on medium speed, beat until the topping is thickened and resembles stiff whipped cream. Make sure no lumps remain. Transfer to a small serving dish, cover, and refrigerate.

3. Transfer the cooked fruit to a serving bowl and let cool until warm. Or chill in the refrigerator, if desired.

4. To serve, spoon the compote into individual glass serving dishes and garnish with the topping.

ADVANCE PREPARATION:
Make up to 1 day ahead through step 3, cover, and refrigerate.

DOUBLE-PERSIMMON PUDDING

This version of my persimmon pudding from *The Cuisine of California* shows off two decidedly different varieties. Astringent Hachiyas, elongated, with a pointed tip, need to become very soft before using. Puréed, they are the base for the pudding. Ripe Fuyus, resembling squat tomatoes, are chopped and added for extra persimmon texture and flavor. The pudding has a permanent place on my dessert sideboard for Thanksgiving. I like to serve it with whipped cream, crème fraîche, or softened French vanilla ice cream to temper the sweetness.

INGREDIENTS:

1½ CUPS ALL PURPOSE FLOUR

1 TEASPOON BAKING POWDER

1 TEASPOON BAKING SODA

¼ TEASPOON SALT

1 TABLESPOON PUMPKIN PIE SPICE

PINCH FRESHLY GRATED NUTMEG

3 LARGE OR 4 MEDIUM RIPE HACHIYA PERSIMMONS

2 LARGE EGGS

¾ CUP GRANULATED SUGAR

¼ CUP PACKED BROWN SUGAR

1½ CUPS HALF-AND-HALF

1 TEASPOON VANILLA EXTRACT

¼ CUP (½ STICK) UNSALTED BUTTER, MELTED

2 FUYU PERSIMMONS, PEELED, SEEDED, AND CUT INTO ½-INCH PIECES

1. Preheat the oven to 350°F. Generously butter a 9-by-13-by-2-inch baking dish.

2. In a medium bowl, whisk together the flour, baking powder, baking soda, salt, pumpkin pie spice, and nutmeg.

3. Peel the Hachiya persimmons and remove any seeds. Place in a food processor fitted with the metal blade or in a blender, and purée. Combine the persimmon purée, eggs, and sugars in a large bowl. Stir until well blended. Stir the dry ingredients alternately with the half-and-half into the persimmon mixture. Add the vanilla, butter, and Fuyu persimmons and mix well.

4. Pour into the prepared dish and bake for 45 to 50 minutes, or until puffed and brown. Cut into squares and serve warm.

ADVANCE PREPARATION:

Make up to 6 hours ahead and keep at room temperature. Warm in a 350°F oven for 15 to 20 minutes.

PUMPKIN-CARAMEL ICE CREAM PIE

✳ SERVES 8 TO 10 ✳

Years ago I began embellishing my pumpkin ice cream pie with a caramel swirl. This version of the recipe is now required for the Thanksgiving dessert table as much as the turkey is for the main course. I've made the pie easy to serve by unmolding the pie shell before it is filled, so the slices will cut easily and come right out of the pan.

INGREDIENTS:

CRUST

2 TABLESPOONS FINELY CHOPPED PECANS

ABOUT 25 GINGERSNAPS, GROUND INTO FINE CRUMBS IN A FOOD PROCESSOR (1½ CUPS)

6 TABLESPOONS UNSALTED BUTTER, MELTED

FILLING

2 PINTS PUMPKIN ICE CREAM

4 TABLESPOONS CHILLED CARAMEL SAUCE (PAGE 218) OR FAVORITE CARAMEL SAUCE

16 PECAN HALVES FOR GARNISH

1 CUP WARM CARAMEL SAUCE (PAGE 218) OR FAVORITE CARAMEL SAUCE

1. Preheat the oven to 375°F. Tightly line a 9-inch pie plate with 2-inch sides with aluminum foil.

2. Make the crust: In a bowl, mix together the pecans and gingersnap crumbs. Add the butter and toss the crumbs to blend well. Press the crumbs evenly over the bottom and sides of the pie plate, using the back of a spoon, the heel of your hand, or your fingers. Chill until firm, about 30 minutes. Bake for 6 minutes, or until just set. Let cool.

3. Chill the crust in the freezer for 2 hours. Remove from the freezer and unmold the pie shell onto a flat surface. Very carefully peel away the foil so the shell stays intact. Return it to the pie plate.

4. Make the filling: Soften the ice cream in a large bowl and mix with a large spoon until thoroughly blended and no lumps remain.

Spoon into the pie shell and smooth the top with a rubber spatula. With a teaspoon, dot the top of the pie with all 4 tablespoons of the caramel. Use a skewer to make a pretty swirl or other design, moving it back and forth about ½ inch deep into the ice cream. Arrange the pecans around the outside edge of the pie, pushing them into the ice cream.

5. Freeze the pie for at least 2 hours. When it is frozen, cover tightly with foil. To serve, thaw slightly in the refrigerator for 30 minutes. Cut into wedges and serve with the warm caramel sauce.

ADVANCE PREPARATION:

Make up to 1 month ahead, cover tightly, and freeze. Thaw slightly in the refrigerator for 30 minutes before serving.

CRANBERRY AND PEAR CUSTARD CRISP

✳ SERVES 6 TO 8 ✳

Here is a homespun dessert that has a surprise layer of custard in the middle between the fruit and the topping. I like to serve the crisp on its own or as part of a dessert buffet, garnished with a scoop of French vanilla ice cream. Fruit lovers always gravitate to this dessert, so make sure to include it in your menu if you have guests who favor fruit over chocolate.

INGREDIENTS:

¾ CUP DRIED CRANBERRIES

1½ CUPS BOILING WATER

6 BOSC PEARS, PEELED, CORED, AND CUT INTO 1½-INCH PIECES

⅓ CUP ALL-PURPOSE FLOUR

⅓ CUP GRANULATED SUGAR

2 TABLESPOONS FRESH LEMON JUICE

GRATED ZEST OF 1 LEMON

CUSTARD

2 EGGS

1 CUP CRÈME FRAÎCHE

1 TEASPOON VANILLA EXTRACT

1 TABLESPOON ALL-PURPOSE FLOUR

TOPPING

6 TABLESPOONS PACKED BROWN SUGAR

¾ CUP ALL-PURPOSE FLOUR

¼ CUP FINELY GROUND PECANS

½ TEASPOON SALT

1 TEASPOON GROUND CINNAMON

1 TEASPOON GRATED LEMON ZEST

1 TEASPOON VANILLA EXTRACT

½ CUP (1 STICK) UNSALTED BUTTER, MELTED

1. Preheat the oven to 375°F. Butter a 9-by-12-inch gratin dish or baking dish. In a small bowl, combine the cranberries and boiling water, making sure to cover the fruit. Let stand for 10 minutes, or until the cranberries are plump. Drain well.

2. In a medium bowl, combine the cranberries, pears, flour, sugar, and lemon juice and zest. Mix until the fruit is well coated. Transfer to the prepared dish. Press down on the mixture with a spatula to make an even layer with no gaps. Place on a baking sheet.

3. Make the custard: In a medium bowl, with a whisk, beat the eggs well. Add the crème fraîche and vanilla and whisk until blended. Sift in the flour, whisking well to make sure the custard is smooth and no lumps remain.

4. Make the topping: In a medium bowl, stir together the brown sugar, flour, pecans, salt, cinnamon, and lemon zest. Add the vanilla and butter and mix with a fork until a soft dough forms.

5. Spread an even layer of the custard mixture over the fruit. With your fingers, evenly crumble the topping over the fruit. Bake for about 55 minutes, or until the top is golden brown and cooked through. Let rest for 10 minutes, then serve.

ADVANCE PREPARATION:
Make up to 4 hours ahead, cover, and keep at room temperature. Warm in a 375°F oven for 10 to 15 minutes.

DRIED FRUIT AND CHOCOLATE BAR COOKIES

Part candy bar, part cookie, this holiday confection is loaded with fruit, nuts, and chocolate. The cookies are a welcome addition to the holiday dessert table. You can also cut them into small bars and wrap them as holiday gifts. They keep well because of the moisture in the reconstituted fruit and chocolate.

INGREDIENTS:

1¼ CUPS CHOPPED DRIED APRICOTS

1¼ CUPS DRIED CRANBERRIES

2 CUPS BOILING WATER

1 CUP CHOPPED WALNUTS

2½ CUPS ALL-PURPOSE FLOUR

1½ TEASPOONS BAKING SODA

1 TEASPOON SALT

1 TEASPOON PUMPKIN PIE SPICE

1 CUP (2 STICKS) UNSALTED BUTTER AT ROOM TEMPERATURE

2 CUPS GRANULATED SUGAR

3 LARGE EGGS

2 TEASPOONS VANILLA EXTRACT

4 OUNCES BITTERSWEET CHOCO-LATE (70 TO 75 PERCENT CACAO), COARSELY CHOPPED

4 OUNCES WHITE CHOCOLATE, COARSELY CHOPPED

1. Place the dried fruit in a medium heat-proof bowl and pour in the boiling water, making sure to cover the fruit. Let stand for 30 minutes. Drain well.

2. Preheat the oven to 350°F. Place the walnuts on a baking sheet and toast for 7 to 10 minutes, or until lightly browned. Let cool.

3. Butter and flour a 12-by-17-by-1-inch jelly-roll pan.

4. In a medium bowl, combine the flour, baking soda, salt, and pumpkin pie spice. Add the walnuts and mix with a fork.

5. In another large bowl, beat the butter with an electric mixer on medium speed until light and fluffy. Gradually add the sugar, continuing to beat until very light. Add the eggs one at a time, beating well after each addition. Add the vanilla and mix again. With the mixer on low speed, beat in the flour mixture along with the dried fruit until just combined. Add the chocolate pieces and carefully blend into the batter with the electric mixer.

6. Evenly spread the batter in the prepared pan. Bake for about 45 minutes, or until a skewer inserted into the center comes out almost clean and the top is golden brown. Let cool for at least 1 hour. Cut into bars and serve.

ADVANCE PREPARATION:
Make up to 2 days ahead, cover, and keep at room temperature in an airtight container.

THE CLEVER COOK COULD:
- Vary the dried fruits and nuts by using chopped dried cherries, peaches, or nectarines and pecans or almonds.
- Cut the bars in half and serve in small paper cups as petits fours after dinner.

SOUR CREAM–VANILLA CUPCAKES

✳ SERVES 12 ✳

Author Elinor Klivans knows a lot about cupcakes. This recipe, adapted from her book *Cupcakes*, has received raves from my friends and family who are cupcake lovers. The cupcakes are fun to make with kids, and they lend themselves to decorating for any holiday: use black and orange sprinkles for Halloween, orange for Thanksgiving, blue and silver for Hanukkah, and red and green for Christmas. Use a good-quality vanilla extract for this recipe so the flavor really stands out.

INGREDIENTS:

1¼ CUPS ALL-PURPOSE FLOUR

½ TEASPOON BAKING POWDER

¼ TEASPOON BAKING SODA

¼ TEASPOON SALT

2 LARGE EGGS

1 CUP GRANULATED SUGAR

½ CUP (1 STICK) UNSALTED BUTTER AT ROOM TEMPERATURE

1½ TEASPOONS VANILLA EXTRACT

½ CUP SOUR CREAM

FROSTING

½ CUP (1 STICK) UNSALTED BUTTER AT ROOM TEMPERATURE

3 CUPS POWDERED SUGAR

1 TEASPOON VANILLA EXTRACT

3 TO 4 TABLESPOONS MILK

COLORED SPRINKLES OF YOUR CHOICE

1. Preheat the oven to 350°F. Line 12 standard muffin cups with paper liners.

2. Sift the flour, baking powder, baking soda, and salt onto a large piece of waxed paper.

3. In a large bowl, with an electric mixer on medium speed, beat the eggs and sugar for about 2 minutes, or until light and creamy. Add the butter and vanilla and beat on low speed for about 1 minute, or until well blended. Beat in the dry ingredients on low speed until blended. Add the sour cream and beat until smooth and well blended.

4. Fill each cup with about 2 tablespoons of the batter. Bake for about 23 minutes, or until a toothpick inserted into the center of a cupcake comes out clean and the tops are firm. Let cool in the pan for about 10 minutes. Transfer the cupcakes to a wire rack to cool to room temperature.

5. Meanwhile, make the frosting: In a large bowl, combine the butter, powdered sugar, and vanilla. Using the electric mixer on low speed, beat until the mixture begins to come together. Add enough milk, beating on low speed, to make a creamy consistency.

6. Using a metal spatula, apply 1½ to 2 tablespoons frosting to each cupcake, forming tiny peaks while turning the cupcake. Garnish with sprinkles. Place on a pretty platter and serve.

ADVANCE PREPARATION:
Make 1 day ahead, cover tightly, and keep at room temperature.

APPLE CLAFOUTI

Clafouti is usually made with cherries. This version with apples is just right on a cold afternoon or as a comforting conclusion to a Sunday supper. I like to serve it directly from the oven when it is puffed up. It also makes a delicious finale to a lunch that begins with Green Lentil Soup with Sausages and Red Peppers (page 75) and follows with Winter Chopped Salad (page 80), with or without chicken, for the main course. If you like, garnish each serving with a dollop of whipped cream or small scoop of vanilla ice cream.

INGREDIENTS:

2 LARGE GALA OR PINK LADY APPLES, PEELED, CORED, AND CUT INTO 1-INCH PIECES

2 TABLESPOONS UNSALTED BUTTER, SOFTENED AND CUT INTO SMALL PIECES

4 TABLESPOONS PLUS ¾ CUP GRANULATED SUGAR

1 CUP ALL-PURPOSE FLOUR

1 TEASPOON BAKING POWDER

PINCH SALT

½ TEASPOON GROUND CINNAMON

4 LARGE EGGS

1¾ CUPS HALF-AND-HALF

2 TEASPOONS VANILLA EXTRACT

POWDERED SUGAR FOR DUSTING

1. Preheat the oven to 425°F. Generously coat a 9-by-13-inch baking dish with butter. Place on a baking sheet. Sprinkle the apples on the bottom of the dish and then mix with the butter and 2 tablespoons of the granulated sugar until nicely coated.

2. Bake for 20 minutes, stirring occasionally so that the apples cook evenly. Remove from the oven.

3. Meanwhile, combine the flour, baking powder, salt, and cinnamon on a large sheet of waxed paper. In a large bowl or in a blender, beat the eggs with the ¾ cup granulated sugar for 1 minute, or until blended. Beat in the dry ingredients alternately with the half-and-half. Add the vanilla and mix to combine.

4. Pour the batter evenly over the apples. Sprinkle with the remaining 2 tablespoons granulated sugar. Bake for about 30 minutes, or until puffed and golden brown. Sprinkle with powdered sugar. Serve immediately.

ADVANCE PREPARATION:

Make 2 hours ahead through step 1, cover, and keep at room temperature. Preheat the oven just before baking.

CHOCOLATE-TOFFEE PIE

✳ SERVES 12 ✳

The ultimate in simplicity, this crustless brownie-style pie is a hit whenever I serve it. Adding bittersweet chocolate gives the pie an extra-deep chocolate dimension, and the toffee bits and pecans contribute welcome texture. You can bake the pie in an aluminum pie pan if you are transporting it to someone else's home for a potluck or giving as a gift. I like to serve French vanilla ice cream on the side.

INGREDIENTS:

6 TABLESPOONS UNSALTED BUTTER

14 OUNCES SEMISWEET CHOCOLATE
(60 PERCENT CACAO)

2 OUNCES BITTERSWEET CHOCOLATE
(70 TO 75 PERCENT CACAO)

3 LARGE EGGS

¾ CUP GRANULATED SUGAR

1 TABLESPOON VANILLA EXTRACT

½ CUP ALL-PURPOSE FLOUR

¼ TEASPOON BAKING POWDER

¼ TEASPOON SALT

½ CUP TOFFEE BITS

½ CUP CHOPPED PECANS

GLAZE

1 OUNCE SEMISWEET CHOCOLATE
(60 PERCENT CACAO) CUT INTO PIECES

2 TABLESPOONS HEAVY CREAM

1. Preheat the oven to 350°F. Butter a 9-inch pie pan or plate. Combine the butter and chocolates in a large glass measuring cup and melt in the microwave, 1½ to 2 minutes. Or melt in the top of a double boiler over medium heat until completely blended. Let cool for a few minutes.

2. In a medium bowl, with an electric mixer on medium speed, beat the eggs for 1 minute. Add the sugar and vanilla and beat for 2 minutes, or until thick and a light lemon color. Add the melted chocolate mixture and beat until well blended.

3. Combine the flour, baking powder, and salt on a large sheet of waxed paper. Add to the chocolate mixture, beating on low speed. Add the toffee bits and pecans and beat on low speed until just blended.

4. Pour the batter into the prepared pan and place on a baking sheet. Bake for about 50 minutes, or until the pie has risen and a skewer inserted into the center comes out slightly moist. Let cool to room temperature.

5. Make the glaze: In a small glass bowl, combine the chocolate and cream. Melt in the microwave, about 1½ minutes. Mix with a fork and then drizzle decoratively over the top of the pie.

6. To serve, cut thin wedges and place on dessert plates.

ADVANCE PREPARATION:

Make 2 days ahead, cover, and keep at room temperature.

CHOCOLATE-DRIED CHERRY BREAD PUDDING

Dried cherries add just the right counterpoint to the warm bittersweet chocolate in this comforting dessert. The secret to making great bread pudding is to dry out the bread and let it absorb the liquid before baking. You can put the cubes out on the counter overnight or dry them in a 250°F oven for half an hour. Any leftover pudding is excellent served cold the next day.

INGREDIENTS:

ONE 1-POUND LOAF DAY-OLD CHALLAH, EGG BREAD, OR BRIOCHE, CRUSTS REMOVED, CUT INTO 1-INCH CUBES (8 CUPS)

4 OUNCES SEMISWEET CHOCOLATE (60 PERCENT CACAO), COARSELY CHOPPED

2 OUNCES BITTERSWEET CHOCOLATE (70 TO 75 PERCENT CACAO), COARSELY CHOPPED

⅓ CUP DRIED PITTED CHERRIES

6 LARGE EGGS

2 LARGE EGG YOLKS

1¼ CUPS GRANULATED SUGAR

4 CUPS MILK OR HALF-AND-HALF

1 TABLESPOON VANILLA EXTRACT

2 TABLESPOONS SWEETENED COCOA POWDER

POWDERED SUGAR FOR DUSTING

WHIPPED CREAM FOR SERVING (OPTIONAL)

1. Butter a 9-by-13-inch baking dish. Arrange the bread, chocolate, and cherries in the dish, making sure that they are evenly distributed.

2. In a large bowl, with an electric mixer on medium speed, beat the eggs and egg yolks until frothy. Add the sugar and beat for about 3 minutes, or until thick and lemon colored. Add the milk, reduce the speed to low, and mix to combine. Add the vanilla and mix to combine.

3. Preheat the oven to 375°F. Ladle the egg mixture over the bread, chocolate, and cherries. Let stand for 30 minutes to 1 hour, or until the bread absorbs the liquid. Occasionally push the bread down with a wooden spoon. (To test, cut into a bread cube.) Sprinkle the top evenly with the cocoa powder.

4. Bake the pudding for 25 minutes. Open the oven and, wearing heavy oven mitts, use a large spoon to push the bread down. The remaining liquid will rise. Spoon it evenly over the bread. Bake for 20 to 30 minutes, or until a skewer inserted 1 inch from the center comes out almost clean. (It's okay if the pudding is not set right in the center.)

5. Remove the pudding from the oven, sprinkle it with powdered sugar, and let rest for about 10 minutes. Cut into squares and serve alone or with whipped cream, if desired.

ADVANCE PREPARATION:
Make up to 8 hours ahead, cover, and keep at room temperature. Reheat to melt the chocolate in a 325°F oven for 15 to 20 minutes.

THE CLEVER COOK COULD:

○ Microwave leftover pudding in small dessert bowls for 1 minute, or just until the chocolate melts.

○ Serve with soft cherry ice cream.

○ Cut the pudding with a 2- or 3-inch round cookie cutter and serve on dessert plates with a scoop of ice cream or a dollop of whipped cream, for an elegant presentation.

CHOCOLATE-PEPPERMINT PUDDING CAKES WITH PEPPERMINT STICK ICE CREAM

✳ SERVES 6 ✳

Warm chocolate lava cakes, first made famous in fancy restaurants, are a home cook's dream for an easy dessert. This version has a hint of holiday peppermint flavor, and crushed candy canes add a festive touch to the garnish. Peppermint ice cream, studded with crunchy peppermint candy, is usually available around the holidays. A little scoop adds just the finishing touch to this elegant dessert, which I like to serve at small dinner parties.

INGREDIENTS:

6 OUNCES BITTERSWEET CHOCOLATE (70 TO 75 PERCENT CACAO), CUT INTO SMALL PIECES

½ CUP (1 STICK) UNSALTED BUTTER

3 LARGE EGGS

3 LARGE EGG YOLKS

⅓ CUP GRANULATED SUGAR

¼ CUP ALL-PURPOSE FLOUR

1¼ TEASPOONS MINT OR PEPPERMINT EXTRACT

POWDERED SUGAR OR SWEETENED COCOA POWDER FOR DUSTING

TWELVE 4-INCH-LONG PEPPERMINT CANDY CANES, CRUSHED, FOR GARNISH

FRESH MINT LEAVES FOR GARNISH

PEPPERMINT STICK ICE CREAM FOR SERVING

1. Preheat the oven to 375 °F. Lightly butter six ¾-cup ramekins.

2. Combine the chocolate and butter in a large glass measuring cup and melt in the microwave, 1½ to 2 minutes. Or melt in the top of a double boiler over medium heat until completely blended. Let cool for a few minutes.

3. In a medium bowl, with an electric mixer on medium speed, beat the eggs, egg yolks, and sugar for 4 minutes, or until a light lemon color. Beat in the flour, blending it in completely, and then add the cooled chocolate mixture and mint extract. Mix briefly just to blend. Transfer to a 4-cup measuring pitcher for ease in pouring. Fill each of the prepared ramekins one-half full.

4. Bake for 11 to 12 minutes, or until the cakes are set around the edges but the center trembles slightly when the ramekins are moved. Holding each ramekin with a pot holder, carefully run a knife around the edges. Invert each cake onto a dessert plate.

5. Sprinkle the plates with powdered sugar. Garnish with the crushed candy canes and mint leaves. Serve with a small scoop of ice cream on the side.

ADVANCE PREPARATION:
Make up to 6 hours ahead through step 3, cover, and keep at room temperature.

THE CLEVER COOK COULD:
◦ Chill the cooked cakes for a dessert that has a dense truffle-like texture.

BASICS AND SAUCES

SERIOUSLY SIMPLE SEASONING SALT

❄ MAKES ABOUT 3½ CUPS ❄

This magical seasoning will elevate the flavor of just about anything you cook. I have made a version of this recipe for years and, over time, I have simplified the method by using a food processor. To make this even more quickly, you can purchase already peeled garlic cloves.

INGREDIENTS:

30 PEELED GARLIC CLOVES, ENDS CUT OFF

2 CUPS KOSHER SALT

1 TABLESPOON ONION POWDER

2 TABLESPOONS PAPRIKA

3 TABLESPOONS GOOD-QUALITY CHILI POWDER

2 TABLESPOONS GROUND WHITE PEPPER

2 TABLESPOONS CELERY SEED

1 TABLESPOON GROUND GINGER

1 TABLESPOON POULTRY SEASONING

1 TABLESPOON DRY MUSTARD

1 TABLESPOON DRIED DILL WEED

1. In a running food processor fitted with the metal blade, drop in the garlic cloves and process until finely minced.

2. Combine all the remaining ingredients in a large measuring cup. Add to the garlic and pulse until completely blended. Use a spatula to scrape down the sides of the blender container and pulse again. Transfer to an airtight container or to smaller containers with shakers on the top. Keep refrigerated.

ADVANCE PREPARATION:
Make up to 3 months ahead and refrigerate.

BALSAMIC GLAZE

MAKES ABOUT ¾ CUP

Use the glaze for perking up soups, sauces, and other preparations.
Experiment by trying the different variations to season
complementary foods.

INGREDIENTS:
2 CUPS BALSAMIC VINEGAR

1. Place the vinegar in a small, heavy nonaluminum saucepan over high heat. Cook the vinegar for 12 to 14 minutes, or until it has reduced and become syrupy. Bubbles will begin to form. Be careful not to reduce the vinegar too much, or it will become burnt and stringy. Let cool. Use a funnel to pour the glaze into a glass container with a spout.

ADVANCE PREPARATION:
Make up to 3 months ahead, cover, and refrigerate. Remove from the refrigerator 15 minutes before using.

THE CLEVER COOK COULD:
- Add the peeled zest of oranges or lemons to the glass container, pour in the hot glaze, and let steep. Use on berries, in a vinaigrette, or on grilled chicken or fish. Keep refrigerated.
- Place a few cloves of garlic in the container, pour in the hot glaze, and let steep. Use in fish, chicken, or meat sauces, in a vinaigrette, or on cooked vegetables. Keep refrigerated.

BASICS AND SAUCES

209

BASIC VINAIGRETTE

❋ MAKES 1 CUP ❋

Keep on hand in your refrigerator to use as a salad dressing or as a light sauce for fish or vegetables. You can easily double or triple this recipe.

INGREDIENTS:

1 SHALLOT, FINELY CHOPPED

1 GARLIC CLOVE, MINCED

1 TABLESPOON FINELY CHOPPED FRESH PARSLEY

1 TABLESPOON FINELY CHOPPED FRESH CHIVES

1 TEASPOON WHOLE-GRAIN MUSTARD

1 TABLESPOON FRESH LEMON JUICE

3 TABLESPOONS RED WINE VINEGAR

¾ CUP OLIVE OIL

SALT AND FRESHLY GROUND BLACK PEPPER

1. In a medium bowl, combine the shallot, garlic, parsley, chives, mustard, lemon juice, and red wine vinegar and whisk until well blended. Or place in a food processor fitted with the metal blade and process until well blended.

2. Slowly pour in the oil, whisking continuously or processing until blended. Add salt and pepper to taste. Taste and adjust the seasonings.

ADVANCE PREPARATION:
Make up to 1 week ahead, cover, and refrigerate. Bring to room temperature and whisk before using.

THE CLEVER COOK COULD:

○ Use different vinegars, like red or white balsamic, pomegranate, or other flavored vinegars, in place of the red wine vinegar.

○ Add different fresh herbs such as basil, mint, or cilantro.

○ Stir in 1 or 2 tablespoons nonfat plain yogurt for a creamier dressing.

○ Add diced cucumber, avocado, or tomatoes and use as a sauce for fish or vegetables.

RED PEPPER AIOLI

※ MAKES ABOUT 1 CUP ※

Use as a dipping sauce for artichokes or cracked crab, or as a coating for chicken or fish.

INGREDIENTS:

2 GARLIC CLOVES

¼ CUP JARRED ROASTED RED PEP-PERS, RINSED AND DRAINED WELL

1 TABLESPOON SUN-DRIED TOMATO PESTO

1 TABLESPOON FRESH LEMON JUICE

½ CUP MAYONNAISE

2 TABLESPOONS FINELY CHOPPED FRESH CHIVES

In a mini food processor, process the garlic until minced. Add the peppers and pesto and process to blend. Add the lemon juice, mayonnaise, and chives and process until completely blended. Transfer the aioli to a small bowl.

ADVANCE PREPARATION:
Make up to 5 days ahead, cover, and refrigerate.

THE CLEVER COOK COULD:
- Mix in ¼ cup nonfat plain yogurt to lighten the sauce.

CRANBERRY-POMEGRANATE SAUCE WITH SATSUMAS

❄ MAKES ABOUT 4 CUPS ❄

Cranberries and pomegranates have a natural affinity. Satsumas, seedless sweet oranges, are easy to peel. The combination makes a refreshing variation on classic cranberry sauce.

INGREDIENTS:

¾ CUP SUGAR

1 CUP SWEETENED POMEGRANATE JUICE

ONE 12-OUNCE PACKAGE FRESH CRANBERRIES, WASHED AND PICKED OVER

4 SATSUMAS OR CLEMENTINES, PEELED, SECTIONED, AND CUT INTO 1-INCH PIECES

½ CUP POMEGRANATE SEEDS

1 TEASPOON BALSAMIC GLAZE (PAGE 209)

1. In a medium nonaluminum saucepan, combine the sugar, pomegranate juice, and cranberries. Bring to a boil over medium-high heat. Reduce the heat to medium and cook, stirring frequently, for about 4 minutes, or until the cranberries just begin to pop. Remove from the heat and let cool.

2. Add the satsuma pieces, pomegranate seeds, and balsamic glaze and mix to combine. Place in a glass container, cover, and refrigerate until using. Adjust the seasonings to taste just before serving.

ADVANCE PREPARATION:

Make up to 5 days ahead, cover, and refrigerate. Taste before serving. You may need to add a bit more balsamic glaze.

ORANGE-CRANBERRY SAUCE

I like to think of this as my little black dress in the holiday sauce department. I prefer to keep the sweetness down, so adjust accordingly for your taste. You can embellish the sauce if you like and put your own signature on it. Keep it on hand for accompanying leftover turkey or as a basis for other dishes, such as Baked Brie with Toasted Almonds and Cranberry Glaze (page 60) or Chicken Paillards with Cranberry-Port Sauce (page 106).

INGREDIENTS:

GRATED ZEST OF 1 ORANGE

1 CINNAMON STICK

½ CUP WATER

½ CUP FRESH ORANGE JUICE

¾ CUP GRANULATED SUGAR, OR AS NEEDED

ONE 12-OUNCE PACKAGE FRESH CRANBERRIES, WASHED AND PICKED OVER

1. In a medium nonaluminum saucepan, combine the orange zest, cinnamon stick, water, orange juice, and ¾ cup sugar. Bring to a simmer over medium heat, stirring to dissolve the sugar.

2. Add the cranberries and mix to combine. Cook for about 7 minutes, or until the cranberries have popped and the mixture has thickened. Taste for sweetness and adjust with additional sugar if necessary. Let cool, remove and discard the cinnamon stick, and refrigerate in an airtight container.

ADVANCE PREPARATION:
Make up to 5 days ahead, cover, and refrigerate.

THE CLEVER COOK COULD:
- Add chopped orange segments to the cooled sauce.
- Add chopped, peeled pears or apples to the cooled sauce.
- Add ¼ cup dried cranberries or cherries when cooking the cranberries.
- Add 1 tablespoon orange liqueur after cooking.
- Add toasted chopped walnuts or almonds after cooking.
- Purée the sauce with a hand blender, leaving a little texture.
- Add a tablespoon of chopped crystallized ginger with the cranberries.

MAPLE-PEAR APPLESAUCE

❊ MAKES ABOUT 4 CUPS ❊

I like to serve this compote for brunch, with Potato Pancake Frittata (page 183) or with individual crisp potato pancakes.

INGREDIENTS:

6 PINK LADY, FUJI, OR MACINTOSH APPLES, PEELED, CORED, AND CUT INTO 1-INCH CHUNKS

2 BOSC, COMICE, ANJOU, OR SECKEL PEARS, PEELED, CORED, AND CUT INTO 1-INCH CHUNKS

¼ CUP SUGAR

2 TABLESPOONS PURE MAPLE SYRUP

1 TABLESPOON FRESH LEMON JUICE

1 TABLESPOON PUMPKIN PIE SPICE

Combine all of the ingredients in a large, heavy nonaluminum saucepan. Place over medium heat, cover, and bring to a simmer. Cook for about 12 minutes, or until the apples are slightly softened. Uncover and cook, stirring occasionally to break up the large pieces, for 7 to 10 minutes, or until the apples are soft but retain some texture. (You can use a potato masher, if needed, to break up the chunks.) Taste and adjust the flavor with more maple syrup or lemon juice. Let cool and refrigerate.

ADVANCE PREPARATION:
Make up to 1 week ahead, cover, and refrigerate.

WARM SPICED PERSIMMON COMPOTE

❋ MAKES ABOUT 1 CUP ❋

Make sure to use sweet, crisp Fuyu persimmons in this recipe.
They should be firm and give slightly when touched. Serve this luscious
fruit compote on French vanilla ice cream or as a companion to
Panettone Breakfast Pudding with Eggnog Custard (page 88) or
Spiced Pumpkin Waffles (page 87).

INGREDIENTS:

1 CUP WATER

3 TABLESPOONS PACKED BROWN
SUGAR

1 TEASPOON PUMPKIN PIE SPICE

4 FUYU PERSIMMONS, PEELED,
SEEDED, AND CUT INTO 1-INCH PIECES

1 TEASPOON VANILLA EXTRACT

1. In a medium nonaluminum saucepan, combine the water, sugar, and pumpkin pie spice. Bring to a boil over medium-high heat, stirring to dissolve the sugar.

2. Add the persimmons, stir to coat, cover, reduce the heat to medium-low, and cook for about 10 minutes, or until slightly softened. Watch carefully and add more water if necessary. Remove from the heat and add the vanilla. Stir to combine. Serve warm.

ADVANCE PREPARATION:
Make up to 3 days ahead, cover, and refrigerate. Reheat gently over medium heat.

MAKE-AHEAD TURKEY GRAVY

✻ MAKES ABOUT 4 TO 5 CUPS ✻

A large part of being a Seriously Simple cook is thinking and doing tasks ahead whenever possible. This method for making gravy cuts down on last-minute cooking time since the bulk of the work is done in advance. You just have to add the defatted pan drippings from the turkey, which will give the gravy a rich turkey flavor, then heat the gravy and serve.

INGREDIENTS:

½ CUP (1 STICK) UNSALTED BUTTER

½ CUP ALL-PURPOSE FLOUR

4 CUPS EASY TURKEY STOCK (FACING PAGE), DEFATTED AND WARMED

½ CUP DRY RED WINE

SALT AND FRESHLY GROUND BLACK PEPPER

1 TO 2 CUPS DRIPPINGS FROM A ROAST TURKEY

1. In a large, heavy saucepan, melt the butter over medium heat, watching carefully so it does not burn. Add the flour slowly and whisk briskly until bubbles form. Continue whisking for a few minutes until the mixture thickens and turns golden brown. The color of the roux is important, because it determines the final color of the sauce.

2. Add the stock and wine and whisk until the roux is completely blended into the liquid. Continue cooking the gravy over medium heat for 15 to 20 minutes, or until it is thickened and no flour taste remains. Season with salt and pepper.

3. After you remove the turkey from the oven, strain the pan drippings into a fat separator and pour the defatted drippings into the gravy. Warm the gravy over medium heat and season to taste. If the gravy is too thin, increase the heat and reduce the gravy to the desired thickness. If desired, add one of the additions listed below.

ADVANCE PREPARATION:
Make up to 2 days ahead through step 2, cover, and refrigerate. Reheat gently.

THE CLEVER COOK COULD:
- Add ½ cup cooked chopped giblets, ½ cup sautéed mushrooms, or ½ cup diced roasted chestnuts.
- Replace the red wine with Cognac, port, or sherry.
- Use a good-quality vegetable broth instead of the Easy Turkey Stock, and omit the turkey drippings, for a vegetarian version.

EASY TURKEY STOCK

MAKES ABOUT 6 CUPS

Okay, I know what you are thinking. When it comes to making good turkey gravy, the key is using a full-flavored stock, so how can homemade stock be in a Seriously Simple cookbook? But in a nod to convenience, this stock relies on prepared chicken broth combined with browned turkey necks and backs, to produce a semi-homemade version of turkey stock. Although the cooking time may seem long, the actual prep time is remarkably brief. Make this on a lazy afternoon or after dinner when you need to be around the house.

INGREDIENTS:

1 TABLESPOON OLIVE OIL

4 POUNDS TURKEY NECKS AND BACKS

ONE 32-OUNCE CARTON LOW-SODIUM CHICKEN BROTH

2 QUARTS WATER (32 OUNCES)

SALT

1. Heat the oil in a 6-quart stock-pot over medium-high heat. Brown the turkey pieces, turning them with tongs, for about 10 minutes. Add the broth and water, which should come up almost to the top of the pot. Slowly bring to a boil over medium-high heat, uncovered. Remove the scum from the stock with a slotted spoon. Turn down the heat as low as possible and simmer for about 2 hours, or until the stock has reduced by half. Add salt to taste.

2. Strain the stock through a colander or strainer into a plastic container. Let it cool, cover and refrigerate. When chilled, with a large spoon remove the fat from the surface and discard it.

ADVANCE PREPARATION:

Make 3 days ahead and refrigerate. If not used within 3 days, the stock should be frozen; defrost and boil before using. It can be frozen for 2 months.

BASICS AND SAUCES

217

CARAMEL SAUCE

❋ MAKES ABOUT 1 CUP ❋

I adore this dessert sauce. Try it on French vanilla or pumpkin ice cream with toasted or candied nuts on top. Or for a special Thanksgiving dessert, use the sauce in Pumpkin-Caramel Ice Cream Pie (page 195).

INGREDIENTS:

1 CUP SUGAR

¼ CUP WATER

1 CUP HEAVY CREAM

1 TEASPOON VANILLA EXTRACT

1. In a medium, heavy saucepan, combine the sugar and water. Do not use a dark-colored pan, or you will not be able to see the color of the caramel. Dissolve the sugar in the water over low heat. Raise the heat to high and continually swirl the pan over the heat. The mixture will be bubbly. If sugar crystals form on the sides of the pan, cover it for 1 minute to dissolve them. Boil the mixture for 5 to 8 minutes, or until it turns dark golden brown. Watch carefully, as the caramel can burn easily, and if it continues to cook, it will become too dark and taste burnt.

2. Remove from the heat and let the caramel cool slightly, making sure it is still liquid. Return to low heat and add the cream and vanilla, stirring constantly. The sauce may look separated, but continue to whisk, and it will become smooth in a few minutes.

ADVANCE PREPARATION:
Make up to 5 days ahead, cover, and refrigerate.

Table of Equivalents

The exact equivalents in the following tables have been rounded for convenience.

LIQUID/DRY MEASUREMENTS

U.S.	METRIC
¼ teaspoon	1.25 milliliters
½ teaspoon	2.5 milliliters
1 teaspoon	5 milliliters
1 tablespoon (3 teaspoons)	15 milliliters
1 fluid ounce (2 tablespoons)	30 milliliters
¼ cup	60 milliliters
⅓ cup	80 milliliters
½ cup	120 milliliters
1 cup	240 milliliters
1 pint (2 cups)	480 milliliters
1 quart (4 cups; 32 ounces)	960 milliliters
1 gallon (4 quarts)	3.84 liters

U.S.	METRIC
1 ounce (by weight)	28 grams
1 pound	448 grams
2.2 pounds	1 kilogram

LENGTHS

U.S.	METRIC
⅛ inch	3 millimeters
¼ inch	6 millimeters
½ inch	12 millimeters
1 inch	2.5 centimeters

OVEN TEMPERATURES

FAHRENHEIT	CELSIUS	GAS
250	120	½
275	140	1
300	150	2
325	160	3
350	180	4
375	190	5
400	200	6
425	220	7
450	230	8
475	240	9
500	260	10